O9-BUC-158

Modern Critical Interpretations

George Bernard Shaw's Pygmalion

Modern Critical Interpretations

The Oresteia
Beowulf
The General Prologue to The Canterbury Tales
The Pardoner's Tale
The Knight's Tale
The Divine Comedy
Exodus
Genesis
The Gospels
The Iliad
The Book of Job
Volpone
Doctor Faustus
The Revelation of St. John the Divine
The Song of Songs
Oedipus Rex
The Aeneid
The Duchess of Malfi
Antony and Cleopatra
As You Like It
Coriolanus
Hamlet
Henry IV, Part I
Henry IV, Part II
Henry V
Julius Caesar
King Lear
Macbeth
Measure for Measure
The Merchant of Venice
A Midsummer Night's Dream
Much Ado About Nothing
Othello
Richard II
Richard III
The Sonnets
Taming of the Shrew
The Tempest
Twelfth Night
The Winter's Tale
Emma
Mansfield Park
Pride and Prejudice
The Life of Samuel Johnson
Moll Flanders
Robinson Crusoe
Tom Jones
The Beggar's Opera
Gray's Elegy
Paradise Lost
The Rape of the Lock
Tristram Shandy
Gulliver's Travels
Evelina
The Marriage of Heaven and Hell
Songs of Innocence and Experience
Jane Eyre
Wuthering Heights
Don Juan
The Rime of the Ancient Mariner
Bleak House
David Copperfield
Hard Times
A Tale of Two Cities
Middlemarch
The Mill on the Floss
Jude the Obscure
The Mayor of Casterbridge
The Return of the Native
Tess of the D'Urbervilles
The Odes of Keats
Frankenstein
Vanity Fair
Barchester Towers
The Prelude
The Red Badge of Courage
The Scarlet Letter
The Ambassadors
Daisy Miller, The Turn of the Screw, and Other Tales
The Portrait of a Lady
Billy Budd, Benito Cereno, Bartleby the Scrivener, and Other Tales
Moby-Dick
The Tales of Poe
Walden
Adventures of Huckleberry Finn
The Life of Frederick Douglass
Heart of Darkness
Lord Jim
Nostromo
A Passage to India
Dubliners
A Portrait of the Artist as a Young Man
Ulysses
Kim
The Rainbow
Sons and Lovers
Women in Love
1984
Major Barbara
Man and Superman
Pygmalion
St. Joan
The Playboy of the Western World
The Importance of Being Earnest
Mrs. Dalloway
To the Lighthouse
My Antonia
An American Tragedy
Murder in the Cathedral
The Waste Land
Absalom, Absalom!
Light in August
Sanctuary
The Sound and the Fury
The Great Gatsby
A Farewell to Arms
The Sun Also Rises
Arrowsmith
Lolita
The Iceman Cometh
Long Day's Journey Into Night
The Grapes of Wrath
Miss Lonelyhearts
The Glass Menagerie
A Streetcar Named Desire
Their Eyes Were Watching God
Native Son
Waiting for Godot
Herzog
All My Sons
Death of a Salesman
Gravity's Rainbow
All the King's Men
The Left Hand of Darkness
The Brothers Karamazov
Crime and Punishment
Madame Bovary
The Interpretation of Dreams
The Castle
The Metamorphosis
The Trial
Man's Fate
The Magic Mountain
Montaigne's Essays
Remembrance of Things Past
The Red and the Black
Anna Karenina
War and Peace

These and other titles in preparation

Modern Critical Interpretations

George Bernard Shaw's
Pygmalion

Edited and with an introduction by
Harold Bloom
Sterling Professor of the Humanities
Yale University

Chelsea House Publishers ◇ 1988
NEW YORK ◇ NEW HAVEN ◇ PHILADELPHIA

345 Whitney Avenue, New Haven, CT 06511
95 Madison Avenue, New York, NY 10016
5068B West Chester Pike, Edgemont, PA 19028

Printed and bound in the United States of America

10 9 8 7 6 5 4 3 2 1

∞ The paper used in this publication meets the minimum requirements of the American National Standard for Permanence of Paper for Printed Library Materials, Z39.48–1984.

Library of Congress Cataloging-in-Publication Data
George Bernard Shaw's Pygmalion / edited and with an
introduction by Harold Bloom.
p. cm. — (Modern critical interpretations)
Bibliography: p.
Includes index.
ISBN 1–555–46029–1 (alk. paper) : $19.95
1. Shaw, Bernard, 1856–1950. Pygmalion. 2. Pygmalion
(Greek mythology) in literature. I. Bloom, Harold.
II. Series.
PR5363.P83G46 1988
822′.912—dc19 87–18362
CIP

Contents

Editor's Note

This book brings together a representative selection of the best critical interpretations of George Bernard Shaw's *Pygmalion*. The critical essays are reprinted here in the chronological sequence of their original publication, with the exception of the final essay. I am grateful to Marena Fisher for her skill and erudition in helping me to edit this volume.

My introduction argues that *Pygmalion* is Shaw's masterpiece, and that it remains Higgins's play, even though Eliza is the more sympathetic character. Eric Bentley, still the best of Shavian critics, begins the chronological sequence with his strong emphasis that *Pygmalion* is "a personal play," which implies that Shaw himself is its true hero.

Nigel Alexander, in an overview of the play, centers upon the *agon* of ideas in *Pygmalion*. With an eye to the film and musical versions, Louis Crompton reflects upon the difficulties of "improving" *Pygmalion*.

Charles A. Berst's reading shows how elements of classical myth, folktale, and romance intermingle in the comedy. With Lisë Pedersen's comparison of *Pygmalion* and Shakespeare's *Taming of the Shrew,* we enter the realm of contemporary feminist concerns. Pedersen simplifies Shakespeare in a Shavian way, and shows how Shaw rewrites Shakespeare, almost from a feminist perspective.

Errol Durbach contrasts Shaw and Ibsen, particularly on revisions of the Pygmalion myth, while Arthur Ganz analyzes the problematic ending of Shaw's comedy, with some shrewd observations upon the childishness of Higgins.

This volume concludes with Arnold Silver's excursus on Shaw's revenge upon the actress Stella Campbell after the termination of their love affair. Silver gives us Shaw's preface, postscript, and final scene revisions to *Pygmalion* as a curious, almost grotesque psychodrama, both written and acted out by George Bernard Shaw.

Introduction

I

"With the single exception of Homer there is no eminent writer, not even Sir Walter Scott, whom I despise so entirely as I despise Shakespear when I measure my mind against his." Shaw, obsessive polemicist, would write anything, even that unfortunate sentence. No critic would wish to measure Shaw's mind against Shakespeare's, particularly since originality was hardly Shaw's strength. Shavian ideas are quarried from Schopenhauer, Nietzsche, Ibsen, Wagner, Ruskin, Samuel Butler, Shelley, Carlyle, Marx (more or less), William Morris, Lamarck, Bergson—the list could be extended. Though an intellectual dramatist, Shaw essentially popularized the concepts and images of others. He continues to hold the stage and might appear to have earned his reputation of being the principal writer of English comic drama since Shakespeare. Yet his limitations are disconcerting, and the experience of rereading even his most famous plays, after many years away from them, is disappointingly mixed. They are much more than period pieces, but they hardly seem to be for all time. No single comedy by Shaw matches Wilde's *Importance of Being Earnest* or the tragic farces of Beckett.

Eric Bentley best demonstrated that Shaw viewed himself as a prose prophet in direct succession to Carlyle, Ruskin, and Morris. This is the Shaw of the prefaces, of *Essays in Fabian Socialism,* of *Doctors' Delusions, Crude Criminology, Sham Education.* Only the prefaces to the plays are still read, and of course they are not really prefaces to the plays. They expound Shaw's very odd personal religion, the rather cold worship of Creative Evolution. Of this religion, one can say that it is no more bizarre than most, and less distasteful than many, but it is still quite grotesque. To judge religions by aesthetic criteria may seem perverse, but what others are relevant for poems, plays, stories, novels, personal essays? By any aesthetic standard, Shaw's heretical faith is considerably less interesting or impressive than D. H. Lawrence's barbaric vitalism in *The Plumed Serpent* or even Thomas Hardy's negative homage to the Immanent Will in *The Dynasts*.

G. K. Chesterton, in his book on Shaw (1909), observed that the heroine of *Major Barbara*

> ends by suggesting that she will serve God without personal hope, so that she may owe nothing to God and He owe everything to her. It does not seem to strike her that if God owes everything to her He is not God. These things affect me merely as tedious perversions of a phrase. It is as if you said, "I will never have a father unless I have begotten him."

"He who is willing to do the work gives birth to his own father," Kierkegaard wrote, and Nietzsche mused: "If one hasn't had a good father, then it is necessary to invent one." Shaw was neither a Darwinian nor a Freudian and I think he was a bad Nietzschean, who had misread rather weakly the sage of *Zarathustra*. But in his life he had suffered an inadequate father and certainly he was willing to do the work. Like his own Major Barbara, he wished to have a God who would owe everything to G. B. S. That requires a writer to possess superb mythopoeic powers, and fortunately for Shaw his greatest literary strength was as an inventor of new myths. Shaw endures in a high literary sense and remains eminently readable as well as actable because of his mythmaking faculty, a power he shared with Blake and Shelley, Wagner and Ibsen. He was not a stylist, not a thinker, not a psychologist, and utterly lacked even an iota of the uncanny Shakespearean ability to represent character and personality with overwhelming persuasiveness. His dialogue is marred by his garrulous tendencies, and the way he embodied his ideas is too often wearisomely simplistic. And yet his dramas linger in us because his beings transcend their inadequate status as representations of the human, with which he was hopelessly impatient anyway. They suggest something more obsessive than daily life, something that moves and has its being in the cosmos we learn to call Shavian, a comic version of Schopenhauer's terrible world dominated by the remorseless Will to Live.

As a critic, Shaw was genial only where he was not menaced, and he felt deeply menaced by the Aesthetic vision, of which his socialism never quite got free. Like Oscar Wilde and Wilde's mentor Walter Pater, Shaw was the direct descendant of Ruskin, and his animus against Wilde and Pater reflects the anxiety of an ambitious son toward rival claimants to a heritage. Pater insisted upon style, as did Wilde, and Shaw has no style to speak of, not much more, say, than Eugene O'Neill. Reviewing Wilde's *An Ideal Husband* on January 12, 1895, for Frank Harris's *Saturday Review,* Shaw was both generous and just:

> Mr. Wilde, an arch-artist, is so colossally lazy that he trifles even with the work by which an artist escapes work. He distils the very quintessence, and gets as product plays which are so unapproachably playful that they are the delight of every playgoer with twopenn'orth of brains.

A month later, confronted by *The Importance of Being Earnest: A Trivial Comedy for Serious People,* Shaw lost his composure, his generosity, and his sense of critical justice:

> I cannot say that I greatly cared for The Importance of Being Earnest. It amused me, of course; but unless comedy touches me as well as amuses me, it leaves me with a sense of having wasted my evening. I go to the theatre to be moved to laughter, not to be tickled or bustled into it; and that is why, though I laugh as much as anybody at a farcical comedy, I am out of spirits before the end of the second act, and out of temper before the end of the third, my miserable mechanical laughter intensifying these symptoms at every outburst. If the public ever becomes intelligent enough to know when it is really enjoying itself and when it is not, there will be an end of farcical comedy. Now in The Importance of Being Earnest there is plenty of this rib-tickling: for instance, the lies, the deceptions, the cross purposes, the sham mourning, the christening of the two grown-up men, the muffin eating, and so forth. These could only have been raised from the farcical plane by making them occur to characters who had, like Don Quixote, convinced us of their reality and obtained some hold on our sympathy. But that unfortunate moment of Gilbertism breaks our belief in the humanity of the play.

Would it be possible to have a sillier critical reaction to the most delightful comic drama in English since Shakespeare? Twenty-three years later, Shaw wrote a letter (if it is that) to Frank Harris, published by Harris in his *Life of Wilde* (1918), and then reprinted by Shaw in his *Pen Portraits and Reviews*. Again Wilde was an artist of "stupendous laziness," and again was indicted, this time after his death, for heartlessness:

> Our sixth meeting, the only other one I can remember, was the one at the Café Royal. On that occasion he was not too preoccupied with his danger to be disgusted with me because I, who had praised his first plays handsomely, had turned traitor over The Importance of Being Earnest. Clever as it was, it was his first really heartless play. In the others the chivalry of the eighteenth-century Irishman and the romance of the disciple of Théophile Gautier (Oscar was old-fashioned in the Irish way, except as a critic of morals) not only gave a certain kindness and gallantry to the serious passages and to the handling of the women, but provided that proximity of emotion without which laughter, however irresistible, is destructive and sinister. In The Importance of Being Earnest this had vanished; and the play, though extremely funny, was essentially hateful. I had no idea that Oscar was going to the dogs, and that this represented a real degeneracy produced by his debaucheries. I thought he was still developing; and I hazarded the unhappy guess that The Importance of Being Earnest was in idea a young work written or projected long before under the influence of Gilbert and furbished up for Alexander as a potboiler. At the Café Royal that day I calmly asked him whether I was not right. He indignantly repudiated my guess, and said loftily (the only time he ever tried on me the attitude he took to John Gray and his more abject disciples) that he was disappointed in me. I suppose I said, "Then what on earth has happened to you?" but I recollect nothing more on that subject except that we did not quarrel over it.

Shaw remains unique in finding *The Importance of Being Earnest* (of all plays!) "essentially hateful." A clue to this astonishing reaction can be found in Shaw's outraged response to Max Beerbohm's review of *Man and Superman,* as expressed in his letter to Beerbohm, on September 15, 1903:

> You idiot, do you suppose I dont know my own powers? I tell you in this book as plainly as the thing can be told, that the reason Bunyan reached such a pitch of mastery in literary art (and knew it) whilst poor Pater could never get beyond a nerveless amateur affectation which had not even the common workaday quality of vulgar journalism (and, alas! didnt know it, though he died of his own futility), was that it was life or

> death with the tinker to make people understand his message and see his vision, whilst Pater had neither message nor vision & only wanted to cultivate style, with the result that of the two attempts I have made to read him the first broke down at the tenth sentence & the second at the first. Pater took a genteel walk up Parnassus: Bunyan fled from the wrath to come: that explains the difference in their pace & in the length they covered.

Poor Pater is dragged in and beaten up because he was the apostle of style, while Bunyan is summoned up supposedly as the model for Shaw, who also has a message and a vision. It is a little difficult to associate *The Pilgrim's Progress* with *Man and Superman,* but one can suspect shrewdly that Pater here is a surrogate for Wilde, who had achieved an absolute comic music of perfect style and stance in *The Importance of Being Earnest.* Shavians become indignant at the comparison, but Shaw does poorly when one reads side by side any of the *Fabian Essays* and Wilde's extraordinary essay "The Soul of Man under Socialism." Something even darker happens when we juxtapose *Man and Superman* with *The Importance of Being Earnest,* but then Shaw is not unique in not being able to survive such a comparison.

II

Part of the lovely afterglow of *Pygmalion* (1912) resides in its positioning both in Shaw's career and in modern history. The First World War (1914–18) changed Shaw's life and work, and nothing like so effective and untroubled a comedy was to be written by him again. If we seek his strong plays after *Pygmalion,* we find *Heartbreak House* (1916), *Back to Methuselah* (1920), *Saint Joan* (1923), and *Too True to be Good* (1932), none of them free of heavy doctrine, tendentious prophecy, and an unpleasant ambivalence toward human beings as they merely are. Fifty-eight and upon the heights of his comedic inventiveness, Shaw reacted to the onset of a catastrophic war with his bitter satiric pamphlet *Common Sense About the War,* which denounced both sides and called for instant peace.

British reaction, justifiably predictable, was hostile to Shaw until late 1916, when the increasing slaughter confirmed the accuracy of his prophetic views. By war's end, Shaw's public reputation was more than restored, but an impressively impersonal bitterness pervades his work from *Heartbreak House* until his death. *Pygmalion,* hardly by design, is Shaw's farewell to the Age of Ruskin, to an era when that precursor prophet, Elijah to his Elisha, cried out in the wilderness to the most class-ridden of societies. Since Great Britain now, in 1987, is more than ever two nations, Shaw's loving fable of class distinctions and of a working girl's apotheosis, her rise into hard-won self-esteem, has a particular poignance that seems in no immediate danger of vanishing.

Pygmalion manifests Shaw's mythopoeic powers at their most adroit, and it is certainly Shaw himself who is still central and triumphant both in the film (which he wrote) and in the musical *My Fair Lady.* Mythmaking most affects us when it simultaneously both confirms and subverts sexual stereotypes, which is clearly Shaw's dramatic advantage over such male vitalists as D. H. Lawrence or the entire coven of literary feminists, from Doris Lessing to Margaret Atwood.

The best judgment of *Pygmalion* as drama that I have encountered is Eric Bentley's:

> It is Shavian, not in being made up of political or philosophic discussions, but in being based on the standard conflict of vitality and system, in working out this conflict through an inversion of romance, in bringing matters to a head in a battle of wills and words, in having an inner psychological action in counterpoint to the outer romantic action, in existing on two contrasted levels of mentality, both of which are related to the main theme, in delighting and surprising us with a constant flow of verbal music and more than verbal wit.

That is grand, but is *Pygmalion* more "an inversion of romance," more a *Galatea,* as it were, than it is a *Pygmalion?* Shaw subtitled it "A Romance in Five Acts." All romance, literary or experiential, depends upon enchantment, and enchantment depends upon power or potential rather than upon knowledge. In Bentley's reading, Eliza acquires knowledge both of her own vitality and of something lacking in Higgins, since he is incarcerated by "system," by his science of phonetics. This means, as Bentley severely and lucidly phrases it, that Higgins is suspect: "He is not really a life-giver at all." The title of the play, and its subtitle, are thus revealed as Shaw's own interpretive ironies. Higgins is not Pygmalion, and the work is not a romance.

That Eliza is more sympathetic than Higgins is palpably true, but it remains his play (and his film, though not his musical). In making that assertion, I do not dissent wholly from Bentley, since I agree that

Higgins is no life-giver, no Prometheus. Shaw after all has no heroes, only heroines, partly because he is his own hero, as prophet of Creative Evolution, servant only of God, who is the Life Force. Higgins is another Shavian self-parody, since Shaw's passion for himself was nobly unbounded. The splendid preface to *Pygmalion,* called *A Professor of Phonetics,* makes clear that Shaw considers Higgins a man of genius, a composite of Shaw himself, Henry Sweet, who was Reader of Phonetics at Oxford, and the poet Robert Bridges, "to whom perhaps Higgins may owe his Miltonic sympathies," as Shaw slyly added.

Higgins, like Carlyle and Shaw, is a fierce Miltonist, an elitist who adopts toward women that great Miltonic maxim (so beloved by literary feminists): "He for God only, she for God in him," where the reference is to Adam and Eve in their relation to Milton's God. The myth of Shaw's *Pygmalion* is that of Pygmalion and Galatea, but also that of Adam and Eve, though as a Shavian couple they are never to mate (at least in Shaw's interpretation). Shaw rewrote some aspects of his *Pygmalion* in the first play, *In the Beginning,* of his *Back to Methuselah* cycle. There Adam and Eve repeat, in a sadly less comedic tone, the contrast between Higgins and Eliza:

> ADAM: There is a voice in the garden that tells me things.
> EVE: The garden is full of voices sometimes. They put all sorts of thoughts into my head.
> ADAM: To me there is only one voice. It is very low; but it is so near that it is like a whisper from within myself. There is no mistaking it for any voice of the birds or beasts, or for your voice.
> EVE: It is strange that I should hear voices from all sides and you only one from within. But I have some thoughts that come from within me and not from the voices. The thought that we must not cease to be comes from within.

Like Adam, Higgins hears the inner voice only, which is the Miltonic response to reality. Eve, like Eliza, hears the voice of the Life Force. Yet Adam, like Higgins, is no slave to "system." They serve the same God as Eve and Eliza, but they cannot accommodate themselves to change even when they have brought about change, as Higgins has worked to develop Eliza, and wrought better than, at first, he has been able to know or to accept, or ever be able to accept fully.

The famous final confrontation of Higgins and Eliza is capable of several antithetical interpretations, which is a tribute to Shaw's dialectical cunning, as he too wrought better (perhaps) than he knew, but then he truly was a Pygmalion:

> HIGGINS [*wondering at her*]: You damned impudent slut, you! But it's better than snivelling; better than fetching slippers and finding spectacles, isn't it? [*Rising*] By George, Eliza, I said I'd make a woman of you; and I have. I like you like this.
>
> LIZA: Yes: you turn round and make up to me now that I'm not afraid of you, and can do without you.
>
> HIGGINS: Of course I do, you little fool. Five minutes ago you were like a millstone round my neck. Now youre a tower of strength: a consort battleship. You and I and Pickering will be three old bachelors instead of only two men and a silly girl.
>
> *Mrs Higgins returns, dressed for the wedding. Eliza instantly becomes cool and elegant.*
>
> MRS HIGGINS: The carriage is waiting, Eliza. Are you ready?
>
> LIZA: Quite. Is the Professor coming?
>
> MRS HIGGINS: Certainly not. He cant behave himself in church. He makes remarks out loud all the time on the clergyman's pronunciation.
>
> LIZA: Then I shall not see you again, Professor. Goodbye. [*She goes to the door.*]
>
> MRS HIGGINS [*coming to Higgins*]: Goodbye, dear.
>
> HIGGINS: Goodbye, mother. [*He is about to kiss her, when he recollects something.*] Oh, by the way, Eliza, order a ham and a Stilton cheese, will you? And buy me a pair of reindeer gloves, number eights, and a tie to match that new suit of mine. You can choose the color. [*His cheerful, careless, vigorous voice shews that he is incorrigible.*]
>
> LIZA [*disdainfully*]: Number eights are too small for you if you want them lined with lamb's wool. You have three new ties that you have forgotten in the drawer of your washstand. Colonel Pickering prefers double Gloucester to Stilton; and you dont notice the difference. I telephoned Mrs Pearce this morning not to forget the ham. What you are to do without me I cannot imagine. [*She sweeps out.*]

MRS HIGGINS: I'm afraid youve spoilt that girl, Henry. I should be uneasy about you and her if she were less fond of Colonel Pickering.

HIGGINS: Pickering! Nonsense: she's going to marry Freddy. Ha ha! Freddy! Freddy!! Ha ha ha ha ha!!!!! [*He roars with laughter as the play ends.*]

Shaw, in an epilogue to the play, married Eliza off to Freddy and maintained Higgins and Eliza in a perpetual transference, both positive and negative, in which Higgins took the place of her father, Doolittle:

> That is all. That is how it has turned out. It is astonishing how much Eliza still manages to meddle in the housekeeping at Wimpole Street in spite of the shop and her own family. And it is notable that though she never nags her husband, and frankly loves the Colonel as if she were his favorite daughter, she has never got out of the habit of nagging Higgins that was established on the fatal night when she won his bet for him. She snaps his head off on the faintest provocation, or on none. He no longer dares to tease her by assuming an abysmal inferiority of Freddy's mind to his own. He storms and bullies and derides; but she stands up to him so ruthlessly that the Colonel has to ask her from time to time to be kinder to Higgins; and it is the only request of his that brings a mulish expression into her face. Nothing but some emergency or calamity great enough to break down all likes and dislikes, and throw them both back on their common humanity—and may they be spared any such trial!—will ever alter this. She knows that Higgins does not need her, just as her father did not need her. The very scrupulousness with which he told her that day that he had become used to having her there, and dependent on her for all sorts of little services, and that he should miss her if she went away (it would never have occurred to Freddy or the Colonel to say anything of the sort) deepens her inner certainty that she is "no more to him than them slippers"; yet she has a sense, too, that his indifference is deeper than the infatuation of commoner souls. She is immensely interested in him. She has even secret mischievous moments in which she wishes she could get him alone, on a desert island, away from all ties and with nobody else in the world to consider, and just drag him off his pedestal and see him making love like any

> common man. We all have private imaginations of that sort. But when it comes to business, to the life that she really leads as distinguished from the life of dreams and fancies, she likes Freddy and she likes the Colonel; and she does not like Higgins and Mr Doolittle. Galatea never does quite like Pygmalion: his relation to her is too godlike to be altogether agreeable.

Shaw is clearly Pygmalion-Higgins here, and Mrs. Patrick Campbell is Galatea-Eliza. Mrs. Campbell, the actress who first played Eliza, had jilted Shaw definitively the year before *Pygmalion* opened in London, thus ending their never-consummated love affair. The price of being the prophet of Creative Evolution, in art as in experience, is that you never do get to make love to the Life Force.

A Personal Play

Eric Bentley

Reviewing Shaw's first decade in the theatre, one can see that, taking up the materials of the theatre as he found them, and enriching them with thoughts and attitudes he had learnt from life and literature, Shaw created a new type of comedy. Compare any of his plays with the kind of play he is parodying or otherwise modifying and his own contribution to the drama will be evident. Were we to have entered a theatre in 1900 the things that would have struck us in a Shaw play, assuming that we were sympathetic enough to notice them, would have been—in order of their saliency—the endlessly witty and eloquent talk, the wideness of reference in the dialogue, the incredible liveliness of the characters, the swift tempo, the sudden and unexpected reverses (especially anticlimaxes), in a phrase, the unusual energy coupled with the unusual intellect. And the gist of the early reviews is that, though it wasn't drama, it was something as serious as it was entertaining, as brilliant as it was funny. The more intelligent reviewers began by gravely observing that it wasn't drama and ended by saying precisely the opposite. Shaw is not a dramatist, says one, but a preacher and satirist—"incidentally, no doubt, he often gives us very good drama indeed." "The chief characteristics of Mr. Bernard Shaw's plays," says another, "are not precisely dramatic," yet he goes on to say of the new drama, "the special mode of its manifestation does belong to the stage." "As a conscientious critic," says a third, "I have pointed out that Mr. Shaw's abundance of ideas spoils his plays. I may

---

add as a man," he somewhat disarmingly goes on, "that to me it is their great attraction."

It all boils down to the fact that Shaw's plays were good in an unfamiliar way. What was new about them? Though this question has been partly answered [elsewhere] it may be of interest to recall Shaw's own answer. He located the newness of Ibsen (and for "Ibsen," throughout *The Quintessence of Ibsenism,* we should read "Shaw") in two things: his naturalism and his use of discussion. The naturalism is arrived at primarily by the replacement of romance and melodrama by "natural history." This entails a vast extension of subject matter. Invariably naturalism has meant an extension of subject matter, so to say, downwards—towards the inclusion of low life and animal passions. Shaw made this extension in his Unpleasant Plays. A more characteristically Shavian extension of subject matter was the extension *upwards* in the Pleasant Plays and the *Three Plays for Puritans,* an extension towards the inclusion of the higher passions—the passion for beauty, for goodness, for control. Sardoodledom had removed from the theatre most of the serious interests of civilized men. Nobody did more than Shaw to bring them all back. And nobody brought them back more entertainingly.

As for the use of discussion, Shaw observes that the conventional nineteenth-century play consisted of an exposition, a complication, and a denouement, but that Ibsen, in *A Doll's House,* replaced the denouement by a discussion, and thus made the essential technical innovation in modern drama. Luckily Shaw goes on to qualify this oversimplification with the observation that the new element of discussion may sometimes be found at the beginning (one thinks of *The Apple Cart*) or in the middle (one thinks of *Man and Superman*) or it may interpenetrate the whole action—one thinks of a dozen Shaw plays. As so often, Shaw's critical comment is too simple to cover his practice. A Shavian play is not to be equated with a non-Shavian play plus discussion. The truth is far more complicated. Shaw is perfectly capable of writing a *drame* which is as personal and emotional as one of Ibsen's. He has also written much disquisitory dialogue. Personal plays—such as *Candida*—and discussion plays—such as *Getting Married*—are, in fact, the twin poles of Shavian drama. Without denying the existence of either, one should see that the bulk of Shaw's plays are on middle ground between the poles.

Another distinction is called for. There are broadly two different kinds of discussion in Shavian drama. The one has become a byword because, until Shaw proved the contrary, everyone denied that it could be dramatic. I refer to the discussion of problems for their inherent interest. "Don Juan in Hell," "The Doctrine of the Brothers Barnabas," *In Good King Charles's Golden Days* are instances. In these nothing is more important than the discussion itself. The other type of discussion is more usual on the stage—discussion as an emanation of conflict between persons. Shaw is expert at writing verbal duels in which the acerbity and the interest derive not from the questions discussed but from situation and character. The discussions in *Major Barbara* and *John Bull's Other Island* are of this type. Of course our two types are again twin poles, and most of Shavian dialogue is between the extremes. It is therefore not enough to say, on the one hand, that Shaw makes the ideas themselves dramatic, for this implies that he eschews drama of character and situation. It is not enough to say, on the other hand, that Shaw after all wrote *Candida,* for this implies that Shaw is at his best only when he is closest to conventional patterns, only when the discussions never venture far from the human crisis that is being enacted. One must take particular cases to see how Shaw is drawn now to one magnetic pole, now to another, and how at his best he feels and expresses tension from the pull of both. To analyse particular plays will also afford an opportunity of illustrating other points that so far have remained mere generalizations.

Pygmalion is a characteristic instance of a personal play. And it is characteristic that many people think of it as very disquisitory. At least it at first seems to conform to Shaw's formula: exposition, complication, discussion. But let us take a closer look.

Pygmalion is the story, in five acts, of Henry Higgins's attempt to make a duchess out of a flower girl. Act 1 is really a sort of prologue in which the two main characters encounter each other. The action proper starts in act 2 when Higgins decides to make the experiment. In act 3 the experiment reaches its first stage when Eliza appears in upper-class company behaving like an imperfectly functioning mechanical doll. Readers of Bergson will understand why this scene gets more laughs than all the others put together, so that to the groundlings the rest of the play seems a prolonged anticlimax. Has not Shaw blundered? What ought to be the climax seems to have been left out: it is between acts 3 and 4 that Eliza is finally passed off as a duchess at an ambassador's party. Would not Sarcey have called this the *scène à faire?* When the curtain goes up on act 4 all is over; Eliza has triumphed. Higgins is satisfied, bored, and wondering what to do next. The comedy is over. But there are two more acts!

"The play is now virtually over but the characters will discuss it at length for two Acts more." Such is the curtain line of act 1 in a later Shaw play. It is one of those Shavian jokes which appear to be against Shaw but are really against the vulgar opinion of Shaw. The two acts that follow (in *Too True to be Good*) are *not* a discussion of what happens in act 1. Nor are the last two acts of *Pygmalion* as purely disquisitory as they at first seem.

Certainly, the big event occurs between the acts, and the last two acts *are* a "discussion" of the consequences. But the discussion is of the second of the types defined above: it is not so much that the consequences are discussed as that the consequences are worked out and determined by a conflict that is expressed in verbal swordplay. There is no pretence of objectivity. Each character speaks for himself, and speaks, not as a contributor to a debate, but as one whose life is at stake. Eliza is talking to free herself. Higgins is talking to keep his domination over her. The conclusion of conversations of this kind is not the statement of a principle (as in Plato's symposia or even Shaw's *Getting Married*) but the making of a decision. Ibsen's Nora slams the door, his Ellida decides to stay at home. What happens to Eliza? What *can* happen, now that the flower girl is a duchess, the statue a flesh-and-blood Galatea?

In the original romance, so lyrically revived by Shaw's friend William Morris, Pygmalion marries Galatea. Might not something of the kind be possible for Shaw, since Pygmalion is a life-giver, a symbol of vitality, since in Eliza the crime of poverty has been overcome, the sin of ignorance cancelled? Or might not Higgins and Eliza be the "artist man" and "mother woman" discussed in *Man and Superman*? They might—if Shaw actually went to work so allegorically, so abstractly, so idealistically. Actually *Pygmalion: A Romance* stands related to Romance precisely as *The Devil's Disciple* stands to Melodrama or *Candida* to Domestic Drama. It is a serious parody, a translation into the language of "natural history." The primary inversion is that of Pygmalion's character. The Pygmalion of Romance turns a statue into a human being. The Pygmalion of "natural history" tries to turn a human being into a statue, tries to make of Eliza Doolittle a mechanical doll in the role of a duchess. Or rather he tries to make from one kind of doll—a flower girl who cannot afford the luxury of being human—another kind of doll—a duchess to whom manners are an adequate substitute for morals.

There is a character named Pygmalion in *Back to Methuselah*. He is a sort of Frankenstein or Pavlov. He thinks that you can put together a man by assembling mechanical parts. Henry Higgins also thinks he has made a person—or at least an amenable slave—when he has "assembled" a duchess. But the monster turns against Frankenstein. Forces have been brought into play of which the man-maker knows nothing. And Shaw's Pygmalion has helped into being a creature even more mysterious than a monster: a human being.

If the first stage of Higgins's experiment was reached when Eliza made her *faux pas* before Mrs. Higgins's friends, and the second when she appeared in triumph at the ball, Shaw, who does not believe in endings, sees her through two more stages in the final acts of his play, leaving her still very much in flux at the end. The third stage is rebellion. Eliza's feelings are wounded because, after the reception, Higgins does not treat her kindly, but talks of her as a guinea pig. Eliza has acquired finer feelings.

While some have felt that the play should end with the reception, others have felt that it could end with the suggestion that Eliza has begun to rebel. It seems, indeed, that the creator of the role of Eliza thought this. In her memoirs Mrs. Patrick Campbell wrote:

> The last act of the play did not travel across the footlights with as clear dramatic sequence as the preceding acts—owing entirely to the fault of the author.

The sympathetic analyst of the play will more probably agree with Shaw himself who, Mrs. Campbell says, "declared I might be able to play a tune with one finger, but a full orchestral score was Greek to me." The fifth act of *Pygmalion* is far from superfluous. It is the climax. The arousing of Eliza's resentment in the fourth act was the birth of a soul. But to be born is not enough. One must also grow up. Growing up is the fourth and last stage of Eliza's evolution. This consummation is reached in the final "discussion" with Higgins—a piece of dialogue that is superb comedy not only because of its wit and content but also because it proceeds from a dramatic situation, perhaps the most dramatic of all dramatic situations: two completely articulate characters engaged in a battle of words on which both their fates depend. It is a Strindbergian battle of wills. But not of sex. Higgins will never marry. He wants to remain in the relation of God the Creator as far as Eliza is concerned. For her part Eliza will marry. But she won't marry Higgins.

The play ends with Higgins's knowingly declaring that Eliza is about to do his shopping for him despite her protestations to the contrary: a statement which actors and critics often take to mean that the pair are a Benedick and Beatrice who will marry in the end. One need not quote Shaw's own sequel to prove the contrary. The whole point of the great culminating scene is that Eliza has now become not only a person but an independent person. The climax is sharp:

> LIZA: If I can't have kindness, I'll have independence.
> HIGGINS: Independence? That's middle class blasphemy. We are all dependent on one another, every soul of us on earth.
> LIZA [*rising determinedly*]: I'll let you see whether I'm dependent on you. If you can preach, I can teach. I'll go and be a teacher.
> HIGGINS: What'll you teach, in heaven's name?
> LIZA: What you taught me. I'll teach phonetics.
> HIGGINS: Ha! ha! ha!
> LIZA: I'll offer myself as an assistant to Professor Nepean.
> HIGGINS [*rising in a fury*]: What! That impostor! That humbug! That toadying ignoramus! Teach him *my* methods! *my* discoveries! You take one step in his direction and I'll wring your neck. [*He lays hands on her.*] Do you hear?
> LIZA [*defiantly non-resistant*]: Wring away. What do I care? I knew you'd strike me some day. [*He lets her go, stamping with rage.*]

With this cry of victory (it rings in my ears in the intonation of Miss Gertrude Lawrence who succeeded where Mrs. Patrick Campbell seems to have failed) Eliza wins her freedom. Higgins had said: "I can do without anybody. I have my own soul." And now Eliza can say: "Now . . . I'm not afraid of you and can do without you." After this it does not matter whether Eliza does the shopping or not. The situation is clear. Eliza's fate is settled as far as Higgins is concerned. The story of the experiment is over. Otherwise her fate is as unsettled as yours or mine. This is a true naturalistic ending—not an arbitrary break, but a conclusion which is also a beginning.

Pygmalion is a singularly elegant structure. If again we call act 1 the prologue, the play falls into two parts of two acts apiece. Both parts are Pygmalion myths. In the first a duchess is made out of a flower girl. In the second a woman is made out of a duchess. Since these two parts are the main, inner action the omission of the climax of the outer action—the ambassador's reception—will seem particularly discreet, economical, and dramatic. The movie version of *Pygmalion* was not the richer for its inclusion. To include a climax that is no climax only blurs the outline of the play. *Pygmalion* is essentially theatrical in construction. It is built in chunks, two by two. The fluidity of the screen is quite inappropriate to it. On the screen, as in the novel, a development of character naturally occurs gradually and smoothly. Natasha in *War and Peace* passes imperceptibly from girlhood to womanhood; Eliza in *Pygmalion* proceeds in dramatically marked stages—one, two, three, four, act by act. Perhaps we never realized before the Shaw movies how utterly "of the theatre" the Shaw plays are.

As we might have learned to expect, *Pygmalion* follows the pattern of earlier Shavian works, not duplicating them but following up another aspect of a similar problem. We have seen how the eponymous character is often the representative of vitality and that he remains constant like a catalyst while producing change in others, especially in the antagonist whom he is educating, disillusioning, or converting. *Pygmalion* diverges from the type in that the life-giver, for all his credentials, and his title of Pygmalion, is suspect. He is not really a life-giver at all. To be sure, Eliza is even more palpably his pupil than Judith was Dick's or Brassbound Lady Cicely's. But the "education of Eliza" in acts 1 to 3 is a caricature of the true process. In the end Eliza turns the tables on Higgins, for she, finally, is the vital one, and he is the prisoner of "system," particularly of his profession.

Ironically parallel with the story of Eliza is the story of her father. Alfred Doolittle is also suddenly lifted out of slumdom by the caprice of Pygmalion-Higgins. He too has to break bread with dukes and duchesses. Unlike his daughter, however, he is not reborn. He is too far gone for that. He is the same rich as he was poor, the same or worse; for riches carry awful responsibilities, and Doolittle commits the cardinal sin on the Shavian scale—he is irresponsible. In the career of the undeserving poor suddenly become undeserving rich Shaw writes his *social* comedy, his Unpleasant Play, while in the career of his deserving daughter he writes his *human* comedy, his Pleasant Play. Those who think that *Pygmalion* is about class society are thinking of Doolittle's comedy rather than Eliza's. The two are carefully related by parallelism and contrast. One might work out an interpretation of the play by comparing their relation to the chief "artificial system" depicted in it—middle-class morality.

In short, the merit of *Pygmalion* cannot be explained by Shaw's own account of the nature of modern drama, much less popular or academic opinion concerning Problem Plays, Discussion Drama, Drama of Ideas, and the like. It is a good play by perfectly orthodox standards and needs no theory to defend it. It is Shavian, not in being made up of political or philosophic discussions, but in being based on the standard conflict of vitality and system, in working out this conflict through an inversion of romance, in bringing matters to a head in a battle of wills and words, in having an inner psychological action in counterpoint to the outer romantic action, in existing on two contrasted levels of mentality, both of which are related to the main theme, in delighting and surprising us with a constant flow of verbal music and more than verbal wit.

The Play of Ideas

Nigel Alexander

Pupil and Puppet-Master: The Creation of a Duchess

The story of *Pygmalion* appears simpler than the complicated intrigue of *Arms and the Man*. An eminent professor of phonetics, Henry Higgins, undertakes, for a bet with Colonel Pickering, a student of Indian dialects, to teach a flower girl from Covent Garden the received pronunciation of standard English and pass her off as a Duchess at an ambassador's garden party. The title of the play, however, suggests that rather more is involved than winning a wager. The story of Pygmalion is told in the ninth story of the tenth book of Ovid's great mythological poem, the *Metamorphoses*. Pygmalion was a sculptor on the island of Cyprus, noted for its worship of Venus, the goddess of love. He was disgusted by the behaviour of the women of Amathus and, as a result, resolved never to marry but to devote himself to his art. He became so proficient a sculptor that he made a statue of a woman so beautiful that he fell in love with it. At his prayer the goddess Venus transformed the statue into a live woman, called Galatea, whom he then married.

Shaw again uses a classical title to remind his audience that he is himself a dramatist in the classical tradition and that this play too is a play of ideas. Shaw triumphantly proclaims in his preface:

> I wish to boast that Pygmalion has been an extremely successful play all over Europe and North America as well as at home. It is so intensely and deliberately didactic, and its subject

---

From *A Critical Commentary on Bernard Shaw's* Arms and the Man *and* Pygmalion.

> is esteemed so dry, that I delight in throwing it at the heads of the wiseacres who repeat the parrot cry that art should never be didactic. It goes to prove my contention that art should never be anything else.

It is often said that Shaw never ceased to be a dramatist even when writing his prefaces and essays. They are, certainly, always written "in character" and there are grounds for thinking that the G. B. S. who was their author was also Shaw's greatest comic characterization. Here, for example, he tells the truth. But he does not tell the whole truth. The play is didactic: but what does it teach? It is clear that the play deals with an important social question and, as Shaw himself said:

> Social questions are produced by the conflict of human institutions with human feeling.
>
> ("The Problem Play—a Symposium")

In this case the human institution is the class structure of society, one of whose most visible and distinguishing marks in the England of the nineteenth and early twentieth century was speech and accent. Societies are always apt to construct class structures for themselves and other peoples' accents are likely to remain as a source of amusement. Shaw, however, was writing about a situation so extreme as to constitute an obvious social evil, one which, as he claimed, could be remedied by relatively simple means. As a practical and efficient man he maintained that the difference between the flower girl and the duchess was a matter of education and accent and not, as the romantics held, one of birth and breeding. Shaw himself, of course, came to take a lively interest in the possibilities of human genetics and was well aware of the important influence of heredity. It was this very awareness which caused him to scorn as unscientific the assumption that the "upper classes" were superior by virtue of their birth.

Few members of a twentieth-century audience are now likely to be shocked by the assumption that if a flower girl is taught to speak like a duchess she will be mistaken for a duchess. As Shaw points out, the transformation happens every day. The actual class barrier which Eliza overcomes therefore appears as old-fashioned as the views of military glory held by some of the characters in *Arms and the Man*. Yet, though the social question has become less acute, the play appears to have become even more popular. There are at least four versions which members of the public may have seen or read. There is first Shaw's original play and it is this play that is discussed here. There is then the film script of the film version made, by G. Pascal in 1938 with Shaw's approval but which differs in some important respects from the play. Thirdly there is the version set to music made by Alan Jay Lerner and Frederick Loewe, called *My Fair Lady,* which was a successful musical and has itself been made, subsequently, into a film. A play is no more superior to a musical or a film than a sonnet is superior to an ode. All are admirable forms of art and may be used by artists as they please. But before anyone attempts to translate one form into the terms of another he must be sure that he understands what the original work was about. It will be argued here that neither the directors of the film nor the author of the musical version understood Shaw's *Pygmalion.*

The film and musical versions do, however, make one thing clear. Part of the play's enduring popularity depends on the fact that it is a variant of the story of Cinderella. In the fairy tale the poor but virtuous girl is transformed for one night at a ball, meets her Prince Charming and turns out to be a princess in truth. This is a story of romantic transformation while Shaw's play is the story of a practical and possible one. The story of Cinderella is a splendid and romantic vision. Shaw suggests that it does not and cannot quite correspond to the truth. One may, of course, prefer the romance and it is clear that those responsible for the adaptation did prefer it, since they have turned Eliza's great test, which in the play is a garden party, a dinner party and a visit to the opera, into the traditional ball of the Cinderella story. It is a pretty story: but you must not call it Shaw. In this play, as in *Arms and the Man,* Shaw was offering his public an unexpected image, and beyond that, one that they are apt to reject. Shaw himself has added to the confusion by trying to force his audience to accept it by writing what he called a sequel to the play.

Pygmalion was first produced on April 11, 1914, with Mrs Patrick Campbell playing Eliza and Beerbohm Tree playing the part of Higgins. Tree had apparently decided to give the play a romantic ending and had therefore introduced a piece of stage business in which he threw flowers to Eliza at the very end of the play suggesting that a love affair was, after all, the natural end to the play. Shaw was infuriated by this stratagem on the part of the actor and consequently when he published the play in 1915 he added his humorous sequel. As he explains in a letter to Mrs Patrick Campbell written on December 19, 1915:

> Besides, I have passed *Pygmalion* for press among the sheets of

> my new volume of plays; and it now has a sequel, not in dialogue, but in prose, which you will never be able to live up to. It describes in an absolutely convincing manner how Eliza married Freddy; how she realized her dream of a florist's shop; how neither of them knew how to keep the shop; how she had to beg from the Colonel again and again to avert bankruptcy; how the wretched pair had to go to shorthand and typewriting commercial schools to learn; how they went even to the London School of Economics and to Kew Gardens simultaneously to learn about business and flowers and combine the information; how Eliza wrote such a shameful hand that she had to abase herself to Higgins to be taught his wonderful Italian handwriting; how Clara was converted by H. G. Wells and Galsworthy and went into a shop herself and saved her soul alive; how the flower shop began to pay at last when they tried asparagus and Freddy became Mr. Hill, greengrocer; how Eliza never got out of the habit of nagging Higgins that she acquired in the fourth act, and, though deeply interested in him, did not quite like him any more than she liked her father, who was rejected by the middle classes and forced into the highest society, where he was a huge success but poorer than he had ever been in his life before on his four thousand a year. The publication of that sequel will be the end of the romance of Sir Herbert Tree; and you will have to play Eliza properly and seriously for ever after which is impossible.

It is easy to see why Shaw wrote his sequel. He was astonished to see his actors and so many of his audience accept, as a satisfactory ending to the play, the image of Eliza marrying Higgins and settling down to fetch his slippers for him. This image is, of course, fiercely rejected in the play but, since the ending of the play is inconclusive it does remain as one possible interpretation of Eliza's actions. Shaw sought to remove this interpretation by giving his own version of events. This was a mistake, and it is a very clear demonstration of the dramatic principle that an audience need only accept from an author what he has managed to dramatize and place on the stage in front of their eyes. Once the characters have left the stage his power over them and over the audience ceases, and there is no reason why the audience should accept his interpretation of their conduct in preference to its own. It is quite clear from his letter and the sequel itself that there is no possibility of dramatizing the actions described in it. The ending of the play is ambiguous for very good and sound dramatic reasons. In choosing to tamper with it himself Shaw achieved an effect exactly the opposite of what he had intended. Instead of confirming his own interpretation it gave a licence to others to complete his play in precisely the opposite way—with Eliza about to marry Higgins. The sequel ought to be treated for what it is—a director's notes to the actors about to play Higgins and Eliza—and attention should be concentrated on the play which Shaw actually wrote.

As Eric Bentley has pointed out in his book *Bernard Shaw,*

> *Pygmalion* is a singularly elegant structure. If again we call Act I the prologue, the play falls into two parts of two Acts apiece. Both parts are Pygmalion myths. In the first a duchess is made out of a flower girl. In the second a woman is made out of a duchess. Since these two parts are the main, inner action the omission of the climax of the outer action—the ambassador's reception—will seem particularly discreet, economical and dramatic.

Shaw wrote his sequel because he regarded the creation of the woman as rather more important than the creation of the duchess and was alarmed that his audience should have missed the point. It is easier to accept the myth which transforms the flower girl into the reigning beauty and to concentrate on the scientific apparatus of phonetics, and ignore the other more difficult transformation—the creation of a free and independent spirit. It is natural, therefore, that any version of the play which seeks to emphasize the Cinderella aspects should emphasize externals, the teaching and the triumphant appearances, rather than the clash of personality between Higgins and Eliza. In the course of the Pascal–Shaw revision, some good jokes have been added. The attentive reader will search the stage play in vain for the lines that, "The rain in Spain stays mainly in the plain," or, "In Hertford, Hereford and Hampshire, hurricanes hardly happen." But to shift the balance of the play in this way is to make it belong entirely to Higgins in his role of grand puppet-master. This certainly makes an acceptable fairy story, but it is not the story that Shaw wrote in which Eliza, in the end, betters her instruction and becomes a more complete human being than her creator and teacher. It seems a fair prediction that, in the long run, Shaw's drama will hold the stage rather than the romantic travesties that have been made of it. They, after all, serve exactly the notions of high romance so bitterly attacked in *Arms and the Man* and *Pygmalion*. In the short run, however, the Royal Academy of Dramatic Art must be grateful for Mr Alan Jay Lerner and *My Fair Lady* since the revenues which he has earned for the Shaw estate have helped the Academy and the British theatre. One may protest at the quality of the ideas, which are not Shaw's, but one cannot deny Mr Lerner's romantic craftsmanship.

From the opening of the play it is emphasized that Professor Higgins knows more, and cares more, about sounds than about people. He is neither concerned nor troubled by the flower-girl's obvious distress when he is discovered behind a pillar in Covent Garden taking down everything that she says. She suspects, of course, that what she says is being taken down in order to be used in evidence against her. She has an obvious but nameless fear of authority and it is this which touches the compassion of Colonel Pickering. That this point was important to Shaw is shown by the Final Orders which he sent in a letter to Mrs Patrick Campbell dated April 11, 1914:

> I give up in despair that note of terror in the first scene which collects the crowds and suddenly shews the audience that there is a play there, and a human soul there, and a social problem there, and a formidable capacity for feeling in the trivial giggler of the comic passages. But until you get it I shall never admit that you can play Eliza, or play Shaw.

The first act does a great deal more than simply introduce the characters to us. It gives the audience a very great deal of necessary information about them. It is, for example, rather hard that a man's virility and competence in the world should be judged by his ability, or inability, to acquire a cab when it starts to rain. Yet Freddy's efforts, which open the play, effectively stamp him for the audience as one of the inefficient and impractical young men of the world. His mother proves both suspicious and anxious to keep up conventional standards in the way in which she cross-examines Eliza about how she knew that her son was called Freddy. There can, after all, be only one ground for her suspicions. Eliza herself shows a cheerful readiness to turn even the rain to her commercial advantage, such as it is, until first interrupted and then terrified by the mysterious figure taking notes behind the pillar. It turns out that the figure is indeed a figure of mystery and arcane secrets, though they are not police secrets as Eliza suspected. The scene in the portico of St Paul's Church is a brilliant introduction to the play because in that small area and within that short space of time Shaw has paraded for the inspection of his audience a small cross-section of English society. Eliza herself occupies one of the lowest grades in that society, but there are still present anxious and sympathetic bystanders prepared to protect her from the mysterious force of authority and the uncomprehending police. Colonel Pickering represents the force and authority of that society used with some charity and humanity of purpose. Freddy and his mother and sister are the representatives of ineffectual gentility, while Higgins himself is the power of the intellect—capable, as he himself proceeds to boast, of undreamt-of feats of social engineering:

> HIGGINS: You see this creature with her kerbstone English: the English that will keep her in the gutter to the end of her days. Well, sir, in three months I could pass that girl off as a duchess at an ambassador's garden party. I could even get her a place as lady's maid or shop assistant, which requires better English. Thats the sort of thing I do for commercial millionaires. And on the profits of it I do genuine scientific work in phonetics, and a little as a poet on Miltonic lines.

This boast is followed by the lucky chance that the man he is talking to is Colonel Pickering, author of *Spoken Sanscrit,* who has come from India to meet Higgins. They go off forgetting the flower girl but the flower girl has not forgotten them, and it is on her intelligence and her enterprise in seeking Higgins out so that he may make good the boasts of the social engineer, that the whole play rests. It turns out that she wishes to rise in society. But society, as we have seen it in cross section in the portico of St Paul's Church, is not a particularly edifying spectacle. It seems, at first, that her ambition must be fulfilled at the expense of her independence. In the end, however, it turns out that she can withstand not only society but even the force of the social engineer. Just as *Arms and the Man* examined military courage and the courage required for the war between the sexes, so *Pygmalion* examines the kind of courage required for the battle that is society and discusses the possibility of remaining a free and independent soul even while belonging to a closely knit social system. Shaw uses his storm over Covent Garden as Shakespeare uses the storm in *King Lear;* both, though in different ways, allow their authors to examine the nature of English society. In *King Lear* this examination is simply conducted in Lear's mind on the heath. In Shaw a flash of lightning accompanies Eliza's entrance, and the wind and rain bring society together in the portico of St Paul's Church. At the end of the act the church clock striking the second quarter reminds Higgins that the ladies and gentlemen who have been occupying the stage are not the only, or necessarily the proper, kind and order of society. The clock reminds Higgins, and his sudden and unexpected generosity to Eliza should warn the audience, that this is a play about charity.

Shaw regarded phonetics and the proper pronunciation of the English language as a serious instrument of social change and, at his death, left money to finance research into phonetics and for the development of a proper phonetic alphabet for English. Shaw, that is to say, had serious and important views about this question and made use of them in his play. The idea that speech and accent is one of the great class barriers is certainly one of the important ideas of this play. It would, however, be a mistake to suppose that it is necessary to read and understand Shaw's views on phonetics in order to understand *Pygmalion*. The study of language and the science of phonetics is an extremely complex subject. Nor is it clear that a phonetic alphabet is the solution to the problems of the English language. A student who really wished to understand these questions would not learn very much about them by reading *Pygmalion*. A complex academic subject of this kind can hardly be grasped immediately by an audience in a theatre, and Shaw provides them only with a minimum of easily assimilated information. In his preface Shaw wrote:

> But if the play makes the public aware that there are such people as phoneticians, and that they are among the most important people in England at present, it will serve its turn.

But he is, as usual, being ironic. The importance of phonetics is only the most obvious, not the most vital, idea in the play. *Pygmalion* can hardly be called a play that expresses any very accurate or particularly profound ideas about the study of the English language. It does, however, make use of some fairly simple ideas about the English language in order to make some very accurate observations about the nature of English society, and it asks a number of questions about the relations that exist between individuals in such a society which are both important and profound. Shaw can be seen making use of simple ideas about language in order to ask difficult questions about human beings at the beginning of the second act.

Higgins and Pickering are represented as engrossed in the study of language. But the subject of the scene is not the hundred and thirty vowel-sounds distinguished by Professor Higgins; it is the entry of Eliza Doolittle. Her imagination has been caught by Higgins's boast that he could teach her to speak properly and she has now come to learn and to pay for her instruction. It is, of course, absurd that, in her ignorance, she imagines that she can pay a shilling for her lessons:

> LIZA: A lady friend of mine gets French lessons for eighteen-pence an hour from a real French gentleman. Well, you wouldnt have the face to ask me the same for teaching me my own language as you would for French; so I wont give more than a shilling. Take it or leave it.

The audience will, naturally, treat this as a joke. They will then be reminded by Higgins that it is not really a joke but, regarded as a percentage of Eliza's income, a serious business proposition. That Shaw took this business proposition seriously may be shown from his own commercial practice, as expounded in his speech to the British Drama Conference at Edinburgh on October 28, 1933. There he proposed that dramatists should license their plays personally to enthusiasts in local dramatic societies on a percentage basis rather than the standard five guineas charged by the regular agents for an "amateur" performance. That is, he felt entitled to ninepence or one and sixpence as his share of the proceeds of a local performance of his plays. If, out of a love of drama and respect for his plays, people had put on the best performance they could and had made fifteen shillings, he did not see why he should beggar them by charging them five guineas. It is exactly this argument which Higgins applies to Eliza's offer. By this standard it is, he says, the best offer he has ever received in his life.

Pickering now offers the famous bet—that if Eliza can be passed off as a member of the upper classes at the ambassador's garden party he will say that Higgins is the greatest teacher alive and will pay both for the lessons and for the expenses of the experiment. Carried away by his own excitement, Higgins repeats his boast of the first act in terms which introduce many more ideas into the drama than can be found in a textbook of phonetics:

> HIGGINS: What is life but a series of inspired follies? The difficulty is to find them to do. Never lose a chance: it doesnt come every day. I shall make a duchess of this draggletailed guttersnipe.
>
> LIZA [*strongly deprecating this view of her*]: Ah-ah-ah-ow-ow-oo!
>
> HIGGINS [*carried away*]: Yes: in six months—in three if she has a good ear and a quick tongue—I'll take her any-

where and pass her off as anything. We'll start today: now! this moment! Take her away and clean her, Mrs Pearce. Monkey Brand if it wont come off any other way. Is there a good fire in the kitchen?

MRS PEARCE [*protesting*]: Yes: but—

HIGGINS [*storming on*]: Take all her clothes off and burn them. Ring up Whiteley or somebody for new ones. Wrap her up in brown paper til they come.

LIZA: Youre no gentleman, youre not, to talk of such things. I'm a good girl, I am: and I know what the like of you are, I do.

HIGGINS: We want none of your Lisson Grove prudery here, young woman. Youve got to learn to behave like a duchess. Take her away, Mrs Pearce. If she gives you any trouble, wallop her.

LIZA [*springing up and running between Pickering and Mrs Pearce for protection*]: No! I'll call the police, I will.

MRS PEARCE: But Ive no place to put her.

HIGGINS: Put her in the dustbin.

Anxious to make a start upon his transformation, Higgins gives orders which are susceptible of more than one interpretation. Eliza hears the phrase, "Take all her clothes off," and, assuming that this can only mean one thing, protests that she is a good girl and even offers to invoke the aid of the formerly dreaded police as preferable to this new menace. The whole of the action of the second act depends upon this doubt about whether Higgins's intentions are sexual or intellectual. Eliza assumes that they are sexual, and Pickering asks directly whether they are. Alfred Doolittle, Eliza's father, also arrives to investigate this dubious situation and extract what economic profit he can for himself.

Audiences, therefore, are right to wonder about the relationship between Higgins and Eliza. It is certainly a major question of the play. Eliza is right to be alarmed since Higgins, by talking as if she were a chattel to be disposed of at his whim, does make it appear that he considers her something which he may use for his pleasure. She naturally interprets her role as that of a prostitute. The irony is that nothing could be further from Higgins's intentions. He is interested in her mind as the subject of an experiment and does not really regard her as having a body at all—or any of the feelings that go with one. This method of treating Eliza may be practical, since Higgins knows exactly what he wants done, but it is hardly humane or even efficient. It requires the practical sense of Mrs Pearce and the persuasion of Colonel Pickering before the experiment can proceed.

Eliza's doubts have also disturbed Colonel Pickering and Shaw continues his investigation of the question when Eliza and Mrs Pearce have left the stage:

> PICKERING: Excuse the straight question, Higgins. Are you a man of good character where women are concerned?
>
> HIGGINS [*moodily*]: Have you ever met a man of good character where women are concerned?
>
> PICKERING: Yes: very frequently.
>
> HIGGINS [*dogmatically, lifting himself on his hands to the level of the piano, and sitting on it with a bounce*]: Well, I havnt. I find that the moment I let a woman make friends with me, she becomes jealous, exacting, suspicious, and a damned nuisance. I find that the moment I let myself make friends with a woman, I become selfish and tyrannical. Women upset everything. When you let them into your life, you find that the woman is driving at one thing and youre driving at another.

Pickering's desire to reassure himself about Higgins's intentions has the important effect of revealing a good deal of his interests and character. The opinions of Professor Higgins are a commonplace of the war between the sexes and can be parallelled in many works of imagination and biography. As Alan Jay Lerner makes Higgins put it in *My Fair Lady:*

> You go to see a play or ballet,
> And spend it searching for her glove.

But the difference is that while these are all normal expressions of the difficulties entailed in living with other people, Shaw makes it clear that Higgins not only means what he says but lives and acts by it. His opinions are not simply a manner of speaking. His views, therefore, require further explanation and Shaw is careful to provide this at the beginning of the third act.

In the meantime Alfred Doolittle, dustman, has arrived to enquire after his daughter's welfare and to bring her luggage with him:

> HIGGINS: How much luggage?
>
> DOOLITTLE: Musical instrument, Governor. A few pictures, a

> trifle of jewlery, and a birdcage. She said she didnt want no clothes. What was I to think from that, Governor? I ask you as a parent what was I to think?

Doolittle, the philosopher-dustman, is a theatrical character in a long dramatic tradition. But he is not here to act merely as a comic character. He has a vital part to play in the ideas of the play. We have said that part of the attraction of the play is that it is a version of the Cinderella story. In order that his audience should not mistake Eliza's story for the story of Cinderella, Shaw has given us the story of her father, Alfred Doolittle, who does really imitate Cinderella in his sudden progression from poverty to wealth. He enters the play because he believes that this progression from rags to riches, the Cinderella situation, has already happened to Eliza:

> PICKERING: I think you ought to know, Doolittle, that Mr Higgins's intentions are entirely honorable.
>
> DOOLITTLE: Course they are, Governor. If I thought they wasnt, I'd ask fifty.
>
> HIGGINS [*revolted*]: Do you mean to say, you callous rascal, that you would sell your daughter for £50?
>
> DOOLITTLE: Not in a general way I wouldnt; but to oblige a gentleman like you I'd do a good deal, I do assure you.
>
> PICKERING: Have you no morals, man?
>
> DOOLITTLE [*unabashed*]: Cant afford them, Governor. Neither could you if you was as poor as me. Not that I mean any harm, you know. But if Liza is going to have a bit out of this, why not me too?

Shaw uses Doolittle to shift the argument from the sexual aspects of the situation to the economic. Doolittle naturally supposes that Eliza is "going to have a bit out of this," and since he can't imagine that she has anything to sell except herself he assumes, especially when she does not need any clothes, that the situation is sexual. If Eliza is selling herself, he, as her father, feels entitled to his cut; but, since he is a reasonable and practical man, he is prepared to make his cut fairly modest. His problem, as he says, is an economic one and he cannot afford to have morals. In this situation Doolittle is used to the moral disapproval of society and his arguments have a certain honesty about them which is bound to be attractive. Here, on one level, is what appears to be a demonstration of the practical life and morals of the efficient and practical man. There is, however, one thing seriously wrong with Doolittle's practical considerations. Eliza is not selling herself, has no intention of selling herself, and, as the play makes clear, will never sell herself. Nor is Higgins interested in her as a mistress but as a pupil.

Doolittle in *Pygmalion* is in a similar position to Nicola in *Arms and the Man*. Nicola had accepted his position as a servant and believed that the secret of being a good and successful servant was to know your own place. This worldly wisdom had carried him some way in the world. Doolittle, equally, accepts his place in the world though he describes his place not as a servant but as one of the undeserving poor.

> DOOLITTLE: Ive heard all the preachers and all the prime ministers—for I'm a thinking man and game for politics or religion or social reform same as all other amusements—and I tell you it's a dog's life any way you look at it. Undeserving poverty is my line. Taking one station in society with another, it's—it's—well, it's the only one that has any ginger in it, to my taste.

Doolittle is an ambiguous figure. He has not time for what he calls "middle class morality," which insists that he obey the social forms of polite society. He is not, for example, married to Eliza's sixth stepmother. He is, that is to say, prepared to follow his natural human instincts without caring too much about what other people think about him. His natural human instincts, however, do not seem to include a feeling of responsibility for anyone's welfare except his own. He is concerned about his five pounds, not about his daughter. Concern for no one's welfare but one's own is a coherent and logically consistent attitude to life which has charms for all of us although we are usually prevented, by middle class morality, from admitting them. Doolittle's is what George Orwell once called the voice of the belly:

> His tastes lie towards safety, soft beds, no work, pots of beer and women with "voluptuous" figures. He it is who punctures your fine attitudes and urges you to look after Number One, to be unfaithful to your wife, to bilk your debts, and so on and so forth. Whether you allow yourself to be influenced by him is a different question. But it is simply a lie to say that he is not part of you, just as it is a lie to say that Don Quixote is not part of you either, though most of what is said and written consists of one lie or the other, usually the first.
>
> (George Orwell, "The Art of Donald McGill")

It is unquestionably a lie to say that Doolittle's attitudes are not part of us. But it would be equally a mistake to overlook the fact that Shaw has provided a number of other possible attitudes in the play, some of which may make an even greater appeal than Doolittle's.

Doolittle fulfils another dramatic function. There is, as Shaw points out in his sequel, a certain affinity between Doolittle's single-minded devotion to the main chance and his own economic advantage and Higgins's equally single-minded devotion to his profession and vocation. Doolittle does not need anyone in the world except himself and Higgins's only real interest in other human beings is in the sounds that they make with their voices. Both Doolittle and Higgins are, therefore, independent in their own way. But they are independent because they do not require, or need, or look for any other human affection. They are therefore either fortunate or unfortunate, depending on your point of view, but neither of them would be particularly comfortable to live with, work with or marry. One, therefore, of Doolittle's functions in the drama is to tell us more about Eliza, since he will find himself in the Cinderella situation, and more about Higgins, since he is equally an independent being though not a free soul. All of these comparisons are made again later in the play. At the moment Shaw is concerned to vary his attack upon the imagination of the audience by returning to his main business of Higgins and Eliza.

At the beginning of the third act Higgins arrives at his mother's house in order to arrange for the arrival of Eliza at one of her "At Home" afternoons as a trial for her accent and deportment. His mother is naturally surprised to find that he has a young woman living at his house and, in the course of explaining the situation to her, Higgins reveals a great deal about himself to the audience:

> HIGGINS: Ive a job for you. A phonetic job.
> MRS HIGGINS: No use, dear. I'm sorry; but I cant get round your vowels; and though I like to get pretty postcards in your patent shorthand, I always have to read the copies in ordinary writing you so thoughtfully send me.
> HIGGINS: Well, this isnt a phonetic job.
> MRS HIGGINS: You said it was.
> HIGGINS: Not your part of it. Ive picked up a girl.
> MRS HIGGINS: Does that mean that some girl has picked you up?
> HIGGINS: Not at all. I dont mean a love affair.

MRS HIGGINS: What a pity!
HIGGINS: Why?
MRS HIGGINS: Well, you never fall in love with anyone under forty-five. When will you discover that there are some rather nice-looking young women about?
HIGGINS: Oh, I cant be bothered with young women. My idea of a lovable woman is something as like you as possible. I shall never get into the way of seriously liking young women: some habits lie too deep to be changed.

There is, no doubt, a sense of "emotional inadequacy" here but the inadequacy is a creation of Shaw's talent and should not be attributed to Shaw's own personality. These lines are, of course, not used when an impression has to be created that Eliza will marry Higgins. *My Fair Lady* does not use them and consequently Alan Lerner is free to bring Eliza on at the end when Higgins is sitting playing over old records of her voice and, turning off the record, softly speaks the words, "I washed my face and hands before I come, I did." Shaw ends his play with mother and son embracing each other. His picture of Higgins, as he says in his preface, owes something to that distinguished phonetician and scholar Henry Sweet. It owes even more, however, to the old, crusted, and absent-minded Professor of popular tradition. The Westminster Bank made use of this tradition a few years ago in a series of advertisements whose punch line was, "Wonderful chap, my father-in-law. Knows all there is to know about ancient China, and nothing at all about the modern world." Shaw, it should be noticed, has, as usual, given popular tradition an unexpected twist. Higgins may prefer the company of his mother to other women. He may be withdrawn and single-minded—but he does understand the modern world. The only gap in his knowledge is his lack of self-knowledge, and since he does not require the affection of his fellow human beings, that is not a great handicap. It would, however, become a fatal one if he married Eliza. For this reason Shaw again emphasizes the relationship between Higgins and his mother at the end of the play; he ends the play, after kissing her, walking about and jingling his keys in a self-satisfied manner just as he had in her drawing room before the afternoon tea-party. Since Shaw was writing realist drama he had no reason to be afraid of showing the way in which people do, in fact, behave. A Freudian psychologist would call it a mother-fixation. Shaw saw no need to condemn what he saw as natural, normal and even reasonable conduct. The world of romance, however, has no room for heroes who are attached to their mothers in this way, and therefore, in a romantic version, Higgins has to marry Eliza to show that he is "normal." The point, however, about Higgins is that he is not normal—he is one of the greatest teachers in the world, capable not only of educating the flower girl to be a duchess but giving the duchess a freedom and an emotional independence greater than he himself possesses.

EDUCATION AND IGNORANCE: THE INDEPENDENCE OF A FREE SPIRIT

That education he can give her partly by teaching her to speak and partly by teaching her grammar. In the celebrated scene at the tea-party where, by stage coincidence, the Eynsford Hills, the family from the church porch at Covent Garden, are also present, the audience observes the process of education at a very early stage. Eliza's accent is excellent. Unfortunately she does not yet understand the social and linguistic conventions which govern afternoon tea-party conversation. Consequently when, in leaving, she says in reply to Freddy's offer to walk with her across the park:

> LIZA: Walk! Not bloody likely. I am going in a taxi.

the humorous effect does not depend so much upon the word "bloody" being a mild or shocking swear word but upon the selection of a vocabulary inappropriate to the situation. It is a comic situation of the kind described by Henri Bergson in his famous essay on *Laughter:*

> Sometimes the whole interest of a scene lies in one character playing a double part, the intervening speaker acting as a mere prism, so to speak, through which the dual personality is developed. We run the risk, then, of going astray, if we look for the secret of the effect in what we see and hear,—in the external scene played by the characters,—and not in the altogether inner comedy of which this scene is no more than the outer refraction.

In this scene Eliza is quite clearly such a double character playing against herself. She is both flower girl and lady and the tension of the scene cracks into laughter when the flower girl momentarily overtakes the lady.

There was, however, no such disaster at the ambassador's garden party, the dinner after it, or at the opera performance of Puccini's *The Girl of the Golden West,* which followed. As Pickering describes it:

PICKERING: Anyhow, it was a great success: an immense success. I was quite frightened once or twice because Eliza was doing it so well. You see, lots of the real people cant do it at all: theyre such fools that they think style comes by nature to people in their position; and so they never learn. Theres always something professional about doing a thing superlatively well.

It has not been quite such an unqualified success as both Colonel Pickering and Higgins believe, because they have rather forgotten about Eliza. It is therefore rather surprising to Higgins, coming back into the room looking for his slippers, to find Eliza writhing on the floor and to have his slippers flung at him in rage and despair. It is, as her words make clear, the despair that is the explanation of the rage and Higgins is quite unable to imagine the reasons for the despair:

HIGGINS: Listen to me, Eliza. All this irritation is purely subjective.

LIZA: I dont understand. I'm too ignorant.

HIGGINS: It's only imagination. Low spirits and nothing else. Nobody's hurting you. Nothing's wrong. You go to bed like a good girl and sleep it off. Have a little cry and say your prayers: that will make you comfortable.

LIZA: I heard your prayers. "Thank God it's all over!"

HIGGINS [*impatiently*]: Well, dont you thank God it's all over? Now you are free and can do what you like.

LIZA [*pulling herself together in desperation*]: What am I fit for? What have you left me fit for? Where am I to go? What am I to do? Whats to become of me?

To this Higgins has no answer because it is not a problem that he has thought about or considered. Just as he was not interested in the girl when he started the experiment but made use of her voice and mind, so, now that the experiment is over, he has failed to consider that he has a human being on his hands. He suggests that she might marry and for that Eliza has the most crushing retort in the play:

HIGGINS: I daresay my mother could find some chap or other who would do very well.

LIZA: We were above that at the corner of Tottenham Court Road.

HIGGINS [*waking up*]: What do you mean?

LIZA: I sold flowers. I didn't sell myself. Now youve made a lady of me I'm not fit to sell anything else. I wish youd left me where you found me.

HIGGINS [*slinging the core of the apple decisively into the grate*]: Tosh, Eliza. Dont you insult human relations by dragging all this cant about buying and selling into it. You neednt marry the fellow if you dont like him.

Eliza's point comes with double force because it has been so carefully prepared for during the second act. Throughout that act, first Eliza herself, then Pickering and then Alfred Doolittle were all under the impression that Higgins might be interested in making her sell her body in return for either a home or an education. Now that she has acquired the education, Eliza finds that it has fitted her for nothing except to sell herself in marriage. Education has thus merely trapped her in middle class morality and she despises Higgins and hates herself as a result. She had come to Higgins hoping to change her accent and gain some self-respect. She has gained a new accent but lost her self-respect in the process. For that reason, on the evening of her triumph, she turns upon Higgins and attempts to humiliate him as deeply as he has humiliated and hurt her. He has been guilty of the same crime as her father, Alfred Doolittle. He has used her, or made her sell herself, for his own pleasure. Yet, unlike Doolittle, in humiliating her Higgins has also given her the means to overcome that humiliation. Shaw wrote to Mrs Patrick Campbell on May 15, 1920, that this particular scene "would be better boiled in brandy." He meant that it must be a real fight, not a lover's quarrel. At the end of it Higgins may have won his bet but Eliza has won her freedom.

Exactly how she has achieved this is explained in the course of the fifth act. Eliza has fled to the house of Mrs Higgins, and Pickering and Higgins arrive there in the course of their search for her. They have hardly had time to inform her of Eliza's disappearance when a Mr Doolittle, described as a gentleman, is announced. It is Alfred Doolittle of the second act and he has come to complain about his treatment by Professor Higgins:

HIGGINS: Have you found Eliza? Thats the point.

DOOLITTLE: Have you lost her?

HIGGINS: Yes.

DOOLITTLE: You have all the luck, you have. I aint found her;

but she'll find me quick enough now after what you done to me.

MRS HIGGINS: But what has my son done to you, Mr Doolittle?

DOOLITTLE: Done to me! Ruined me. Destroyed my happiness. Tied me up and delivered me into the hands of middle class morality.

HIGGINS [*rising intolerantly and standing over him*]: Youre raving. Youre drunk. Youre mad. I gave you five pounds. After that I had two conversations with you, at half-a-crown an hour. Ive never seen you since.

DOOLITTLE: Oh! Drunk! am I? Mad! am I? Tell me this. Did you or did you not write a letter to an old blighter in America that was giving five millions to found Moral Reform Societies all over the world, and that wanted you to invent a universal language for him?

HIGGINS: What! Ezra D. Wannafeller! He's dead. [*He sits down again carelessly*.]

DOOLITTLE: Yes: he's dead; and I'm done for. Now did you or did you not write a letter to him to say that the most original moralist at present in England, to the best of your knowledge, was Alfred Doolittle, a common dustman.

Wannafeller has left Doolittle three thousand pounds a year on condition that he delivers six lectures to his moral reform society. Higgins is thus, by an accidental joke, responsible for the transformation of Doolittle from undeserving dustman to equally undeserving gentleman. Doolittle, like Eliza, feels trapped by his transformation. There is, therefore, a repetition, in farcical terms, of the argument between Higgins and Eliza at the end of the fourth act. Doolittle's argument is that in his former state he was able, when he found it necessary, to act as a parasite upon society. Now he is the object of attack by similar parasites:

DOOLITTLE: A year ago I hadnt a relative in the world except two or three that wouldnt speak to me. Now Ive fifty, and not a decent week's wages among the lot of them. I have to live for others and not for myself: thats middle class morality. You talk of losing Eliza. Dont you be anxious: I bet she's on my doorstep by this: she that could support herself easy by selling flowers if I wasnt

> respectable. And the next one to touch me will be you, Henry Higgins. I'll have to learn to speak middle class language from you, instead of speaking proper English. Thats where youll come in; and I daresay thats what you done it for.

Doolittle feels that he has become a slave to his income, just as Eliza feels that she has become a slave to her accent. Nor can Doolittle give up his income and return to his former state any more than Eliza can return to selling flowers at Covent Garden. His transformation, like Eliza's, has therefore worked to his disadvantage since he is now worse off and a less happy man than before he received his income. This argument is comic because it is not possible to feel any great or particular sorrow for a man who has just received an unearned income of three thousand a year. Shaw, however, is using this argument to make another point.

Doolittle has ceased to be one of the undeserving poor. He has become rich but is still undeserving because he does not earn his money by the six lectures a year that he has to give on morals. Shaw is drawing attention to the fact that he saw no way of distinguishing between those who did little, and were poor, and those who did equally little, but happened to be rich because they possessed unearned income. For Shaw the great dividing-line in the world was not between rich and poor, nor between socialists and capitalists. It was between those who did some honest work in the world and those who did little or nothing. And whatever the attractions of doing nothing, Shaw believed that the business of the world depended, in the end, on people caring about, and respecting, the interests of their fellow human beings. Indeed he believed, and often said, that the urge to care for others was not only a normal human instinct but one of the great passions of the world.

There is, however, a great distinction that must be drawn between the morality which insists that one should work and live for others and not for oneself, and the "middle class morality" which is represented in the play by the Eynsford Hills and in which system both Doolittle and Eliza feel trapped. For the essence of "middle class morality" was that the world was divided into ladies and gentlemen and the rest. The distinguishing feature about ladies and gentlemen was that they did not actually do anything to earn their living. Now that Eliza is a "lady" she cannot sell flowers, she can only, like Clara Eynsford Hill, attempt to sell herself in the marriage market. The situation is, as Doolittle describes it, a trap:

> DOOLITTLE: Theyve got you every way you turn: it's a choice between the Skilly of the workhouse and the Char Bydis of the middle class; and I havnt the nerve for the workhouse. Intimidated: thats what I am. Broke. Bought up. Happier men than me will call for my dust, and touch me for their tip; and I'll look on helpless, and envy them.

The problem, however, is not particularly acute for Doolittle. Since he has his unearned income, he can pass from the idleness of the undeserving poor to the idleness of the undeserving rich, and the only price that he has to pay is "respectability"—which in his case means paying out a certain amount of money and restraining some of his natural instincts. If he becomes rich enough and idle enough, as Shaw suggests in the sequel, he will not even require restraint. For Eliza the problem is much more acute. Her transformation has educated her to do nothing and has not provided the necessary cash for graceful idleness. The question then is, "what is Eliza to do?" and it is this question that is asked with some force in the last scenes of the play.

This examination is conducted by cross-cutting the retrospective viewpoints of Eliza and Higgins as they discuss the whole process of her education. The conversation is stormy but very educative for both of them. Higgins begins by repeating the boast which started the whole complicated action and which he has repeated in the second and the fourth acts. Each time it has been repeated, it has been slightly more derogatory, until now he is using it as a weapon of insult designed to hurt Eliza for what he considers her ingratitude:

> HIGGINS: You let her alone, mother. Let her speak for herself. You will jolly soon see whether she has an idea that I havnt put into her head or a word that I havnt put into her mouth. I tell you I have created this thing out of the squashed cabbage leaves of Covent Garden; and now she pretends to play the fine lady with me.

Higgins again shows the tendency, common throughout the play, to refer to people as things. There is, however, a surprise in store, for when Eliza starts to answer him she does so, not by falling in with his bullying and hectoring manner, but by addressing herself quietly to Colonel Pickering. And it suddenly becomes very clear that she has a great many ideas that Higgins cannot have put into her head since he does not himself possess them or even quite understand them:

> LIZA: But do you know what began my real education?
> PICKERING: What?
> LIZA [*stopping her work for a moment*]: Your calling me Miss Doolittle that day when I first came to Wimpole Street. That was the beginning of self-respect for me. [*She resumes her stitching.*] And there were a hundred little things you never noticed, because they came naturally to you. Things about standing up and taking off your hat and opening doors—
> PICKERING: Oh, that was nothing.
> LIZA: Yes: things that shewed you thought and felt about me as if I were something better than a scullery-maid; though of course I know you would have been just the same to a scullery-maid if she had been let into the drawing room. You never took off your boots in the dining room when I was there.
> PICKERING: You mustnt mind that. Higgins takes off his boots all over the place.
> LIZA: I know. I am not blaming him. It is his way, isn't it? But it made such a difference to me that you didnt do it. You see, really and truly, apart from the things anyone can pick up (the dressing and the proper way of speaking, and so on), the difference between a lady and a flower girl is not how she behaves, but how she's treated. I shall always be a flower girl to Professor Higgins, because he always treats me as a flower girl, and always will; but I know I can be a lady to you, because you always treat me as a lady, and always will.

The argument is interrupted at this point, or shortly after it, by the second appearance of Alfred Doolittle in this act. He is on his way to his own wedding and has come to ask Colonel Pickering to be his best man. He has become sufficiently intimidated by middle class morality to marry Eliza's stepmother. His departure for the church clears the stage except for Eliza and Higgins. He now returns to her accusation:

> HIGGINS: If you come back I shall treat you just as I have always treated you. I cant change my nature; and I dont

intend to change my manners. My manners are exactly the same as Colonel Pickering's.

LIZA: That's not true. He treats a flower girl as if she was a duchess.

HIGGINS: And I treat a duchess as if she was a flower girl.

LIZA: I see. [*She turns away composedly, and sits on the ottoman, facing the window.*] The same to everybody.

HIGGINS: Just so.

LIZA: Like father.

HIGGINS [*grinning, a little taken down*]: Without accepting the comparison at all points, Eliza, it's quite true that your father is not a snob, and that he will be quite at home in any station of life to which his eccentric destiny may call him. [*Seriously*] The great secret, Eliza, is not having bad manners or good manners or any other particular sort of manners, but having the same manner for all human souls: in short, behaving as if you were in Heaven, where there are no third-class carriages, and one soul is as good as another.

LIZA: Amen. You are a born preacher.

The argument about manners is extremely important and, obviously, there is as much to be said for Higgins's point of view as for the Colonel's. Both are humane attitudes to the world and their manners are therefore in some respects the same. Eliza's point, however, is that it does not matter that you treat everyone alike, if the way in which you actually treat them implies that they do not really exist and that their opinions and feelings are of no consequence. This Higgins does not and cannot understand. Again he has a defence, and again it is partly true:

HIGGINS: If you cant stand the coldness of my sort of life, and the strain of it, go back to the gutter. Work til you are more a brute than a human being; and then cuddle and squabble and drink til you fall asleep. Oh, it's a fine life, the life of the gutter. It's real: it's warm: it's violent: you can feel it through the thickest skin: you can taste it and smell it without any training or any work. Not like Science and Literature and Classical Music and Philosophy and Art.

It is here that Eliza finds her salvation. She had believed herself unfitted for selling flowers in the gutter and untrained for anything except selling herself in marriage. She has even threatened to marry Freddy in order to escape. Now, however, she realizes that she has the knowledge which Higgins himself has taught her and which she can, in her turn, teach to others. Since she also has some knowledge which Higgins does not possess, and never will possess; the knowledge of how to be kind and civil to people, she will make an even better and more successful teacher than he is:

> LIZA: I'll advertise it in the papers that your duchess is only a flower girl that you taught, and that she'll teach anybody to be a duchess just the same in six months for a thousand guineas. Oh, when I think of myself crawling under your feet and being trampled on and called names, when all the time I had only to lift up my finger to be as good as you, I could just kick myself.
>
> HIGGINS [*wondering at her*]: You damned impudent slut, you! But it's better than snivelling; better than fetching slippers and finding spectacles, isn't it? [*Rising*] By George, Eliza, I said I'd make a woman of you; and I have. I like you like this.
>
> LIZA: Yes: you turn round and make up to me now that I'm not afraid of you, and can do without you.
>
> HIGGINS: Of course I do, you little fool. Five minutes ago you were like a millstone round my neck. Now youre a tower of strength: a consort battleship. You and I and Pickering will be three old bachelors together instead of only two men and a silly girl.

There is no indication that Eliza finds this vision particularly attractive. But as she sweeps out the audience knows that she is indeed as Higgins describes her, a woman, and his equal as a human being. Eliza has found both her independence and her place in the world. Whether she married Freddy, or Higgins, or anybody, we do not know, and it is foolish of the author or his adaptors to try to tell us. What the audience watches as Eliza leaves the stage is a woman on her way to complete her education, and we know that she is both strong enough, independent enough, sensitive enough and humane enough to make an excellent job of it. It also ends the debate on Eliza's education. It turns out that Higgins and Eliza acted as working partners; neither could have succeeded without the other.

Shaw therefore brings his play to an end on something that approaches a note of triumph for the female sex. Shaw himself, in the course of his career as a dramatist, had a great opportunity of observing a number of women who were as free, as hard-working and professionally competent, and as sensitive and humane as any of the men they worked with. It is not surprising that his knowledge of the great actresses and the leaders of the suffragette and socialist movements should lead him to set a high value on the intellect and feelings of women. It is still not a value which is generally admitted by our society and there will be many people, and many women among them, who would prefer to see Eliza fetching Higgins's slippers. Shaw has provided even for their opinions by leaving the question, "what should Eliza do?" as an open one. But in his play he has also provided some of the evidence, economic, social and phonetic, which any audience must consider before it makes up its mind. These problems, of the relations between the sexes and of how people are to live together in society, are not "solved" in the play any more than they are ever "solved" in society itself. The question is always "what must we do to retain our independence and self-respect and yet still treat each other with humanity and charity?" One of the ways in which society entertains and educates itself is by asking this kind of question in its art and literature.

For this reason it is important to examine very closely the way in which the individual artist has put his question. It is therefore necessary for actors, and directors, and critics and students of the arts to pay the closest possible attention to the actual words that Shaw wrote. The tendency to turn this play into a romance comes from the theatrical habit of "playing between the lines." But, as Shaw pointed out to his actors, his plays, like the plays of Shakespeare and other great dramatists, must be played on the lines because it is the lines which make them different and better than the theatrical fairy stories and romances that they resemble. Shaw once wrote to Ellen Terry:

> In playing Shakspere, play *to* the lines, *through* the lines, *on* the lines, but never between the lines. There simply isnt time for it. You would not stick five bars rest into a Beethoven symphony to pick up your drumsticks; and similarly you must not stop the Shakespeare orchestra for business. Nothing short of a procession or a fight should make anything so extraordinary as a silence during a Shaksperean performance.

and he claimed, rightly, that his own plays deserved the same treatment.

If this is done with *Pygmalion,* one finds that what Shaw is offering his audience is not a fairy story about rags and riches but, as in *Arms and the Man,* a number of difficult questions about the education of what Shaw called the human soul. If the audience listens to what is said and considers its own attitudes and answers to the questions, it may find that it understands a little more about itself and the world that surrounds it. Watching Eliza's education is itself an education for the audience.

Since however the human soul may be educated in an infinite variety of ways, there is no final or definite "message" that can be extracted from the plays and offered to the world as the quintessence of Shaw. To suppose that Shaw was posing as a prophet in this way is to misread everything that he wrote about art and literature—including *The Quintessence of Ibsenism.* Shaw offers his audience a variety of entertaining dramatic pictures in which a number of serious human problems are presented in dramatic form and given an aesthetically satisfying resolution. The more difficult the problem, the more difficult it is to provide such a resolution and the greater the need for clear hard thinking and ideas of quality. To expect the dramatist to unlock the secret of life is to expect from him more than he, or any other human being, can give. The dramatist can, however, offer his audience the same experience as Eliza—the emotional and intellectual independence of a free spirit. But the audience can only obtain this experience if they are prepared to work and learn for themselves and reach out beyond the images which, however unexpected, they normally accept, to consider the one offered to them by the artist which they normally reject. For all education, as Eliza and Higgins discovered, is a cooperative process.

Shaw's plays, so far from being emotionally inadequate, are packed with such a range of emotions and attitudes that the critic is in danger of making his own selection only from the emotions and attitudes he understands. Shaw's plays, like Shakespeare's, still have the capacity to surprise us both in reading and in performance. In that surprise lies the secret of their dramatic balance, their dramatic success, and their intellectual supremacy.

Improving *Pygmalion*

Louis Crompton

Pygmalion, as all the world knows, is the story of a flower girl who passes as a duchess after taking phonetics lessons. Shaw himself did not rank this adaptation of the Cinderella story very high among his plays, calling it deprecatingly the last of his "pot-boilers." It has, of course, fully achieved the popularity he aimed at. Its sensational triumphs as a drama, as a film, and as a musical comedy, however, have not been without their ironies. The paperback edition of the musical, for instance, claims to recapture "one of the most beautiful love stories the world has ever taken to its heart." The reader who knows Shaw and the ways of Broadway may be amused at this, reflecting that what the world takes to its heart the world is likely to remold after its heart's fancy.

It is perhaps to be expected that producers, actors, and the general public should have delighted in the fairy-tale aspect of Shaw's play, and have steadfastly repudiated the antiromantic side of *Pygmalion* as so much perverse nonsense from a man who always insisted on teasing as well as pleasing. But the joke deepens when we look at scholarly journals and discover that professors of literature are just as prone as advertisers to assume that Shaw should have let Higgins marry Eliza. In reaction one is inclined to recall gently but firmly such amiable sentimentalists to their senses by reminding them that *Pygmalion* is, after all, not a comedy by James M. Barrie, but a serious study of human relationships by the author of *Caesar and Cleopatra* and *Back to Methuselah*. It is, in fact, just this refusal to sentimentalize that gives the play its distinction.

It must be admitted at the start, however, that Shaw's preface is a somewhat misleading guide to the meaning of the play. There Shaw enthusiastically applauds the new scientific approach to language by phoneticians, if only because it raised pronunciation above the intense self-consciousness and class snobbery which had always bedeviled the subject in England. Then he goes on to imply that the main theme of his comedy will be phonetics. But it takes only a little reflection to realize that dialects, in and of themselves, have no intrinsic dramatic or social significance. Our response to them as pure sounds is largely arbitrary: a Brooklynite's pronunciation of "girl" may strike one ear as exquisitely refined (it did Shaw's) and another as comically vulgar. The real basis for our reaction to anyone's dialect is our association of particular kinds of speech with particular classes and particular manners. Here we are much closer to the real stuff of drama, and especially of comedy. Manners have been a central concern of the comic stage from Roman times through Shakespeare and Molière down to our own day. And, for all the shop talk about phonology, it is possible with a little analysis to see that it is really manners and not speech patterns that provide the clue to character contrasts in *Pygmalion,* accents being, so to speak, merely their outer clothing.

Shaw's opening scene is admirably suited to bring out these contrasts. It is a brilliant little genre-piece that sets a group of proletarians—some timidly deferential, some sarcastically impolite—over against an impoverished middle-class family with genteel pretensions, a wealthy Anglo-Indian, and the haughtily self-sufficient Professor Higgins, all jostling beneath a church portico. The moment is chosen to show class antagonisms and personal idiosyncrasies at their sharpest. Brute necessity prompts a flower girl to wheedle a few last coins from the opera-goers while they in turn face that acid test of middle-class manners, the scramble for taxis in a sudden squall. The scene highlights two kinds of vulgarity. The first is the comico-pathetic, specifically lower-class vulgarity of the flower girl. Eliza is vulgarly familiar when she tries to coax money out of prospective customers, and vulgarly hysterical when she thinks she is suspected of soliciting as a prostitute, on the theory that, as she belongs to a class that cannot afford lawyers, she had best be loud and vigorous in her protestations of virtue. Later, she is vulgarly keen on lording it—or ladying it—over her neighbors with her windfall of coins. What is interesting, however, is that Shaw by no means regards vulgarity as specifically a class trait. All the time he is treating us to Eliza's plangent diphthongs he is also dissecting the manners of the girl in the middle-class family, Clara Eynsford Hill. Compared to Eliza, Clara comes off the worse. For Clara is also pushing, and, in her dealings with strangers, as vulgarly suspicious and as quick to take offense as the flower girl, her rebuke to Higgins—"Dont dare speak to me"—being less comically naive than Eliza's "I'm a good girl, I am"—but just as silly. And Eliza's pushiness at least has the excuse of springing from her wholly understandable desire to escape from the squalor of the slums into a bourgeois world which can offer her some kind of independence and self-respect.

The next day in Higgins's laboratory Eliza is first vulgarly determined not to be cheated, and then suspicious of being drugged and seduced, as the impetuous professor bullies and tempts her. Later, *Pygmalion* reaches its climax as a comedy of manners at Mrs. Higgins's at-home, where Eliza, now master of enunciation as a parrot might be master of it, delivers pompous recitations and spicy Lisson Grove gossip with the same impeccable air. The joke lies in the way the old vulgarian peeps out from behind the new facade, as in her theories about her aunt's death. At the same time, Eliza, for all her absurdity, still manages to think and feel naturally behind the veneer. By contrast, Clara is mere bright affectation, a much less vital person. She even outdoes Eliza's parroting when she repeats her slum expletive as the latest thing. Shaw, who disliked hearing the word "bloody" used "by smart or would-be smart ladies as a piece of smartness," was trying to kill its vogue by ridiculing Clara's callowness.

Shaw's attitude toward manners was not a simple one. Obviously, he preferred social poise and considerateness to mere crudity. He seems even to have harbored some limited admiration for the dignified code of manners of the Victorian period, though he found its artificialities cramping. He gives Mrs. Hill, Mrs. Higgins, and the Colonel exquisite manners to contrast with the girls' lack of them. Yet Shaw is clearly no latter-day Castiglione here or elsewhere. His hero is, after all, the creative rebel, not the courtier. He preferred Beethoven to Liszt, and the rough-tongued Joan of Arc to Ninon de Lenclos. He would have been the first to remind us that on the score of mere gentlemanliness, Charles I would carry the day over Cromwell, and Czar Nicholas II over Lenin. And in *Back to Methuselah,* Shaw's Superrace cannot even imagine what the word "manners" could have meant.

Professor Higgins, Shaw's Prometheus of phonetics, is equally without manners. Consider the Olympian tirade he visits on Eliza's head while she sits snivelling in Covent Garden:

A woman who utters such depressing and disgusting sounds

> has no right to be anywhere—no right to live. Remember that you are a human being with a soul and the divine gift of articulate speech: that your native language is the language of Shakespear and Milton and The Bible; and dont sit there crooning like a bilious pigeon.

Clearly, the man who can vent such splendid wrath upon a street vendor is neither a snob nor a vulgarian, but neither is he a gentleman, and he just as certainly has no more manners than the petulant daughter or the disgruntled flower girl. At home he takes his boots off and wipes his hands on his dressing gown. In creating Higgins, Shaw was assuredly driving at something more than a definition of true gentility.

Before we consider what it is, however, we may pause for a moment to look at the part Eliza's father, Alfred Doolittle, plays in the comedy. Here Shaw turns from the question of social manners to the deeper question of social morality. The farce of the dustman turned moral preacher has always delighted Shaw's audiences. But just as they have rested content with the Cinderella aspect of the main story, so the ironic intention in this second transformation has been missed. One critic [William Irvine] has even held that since Doolittle is less happy after coming into his fortune than he was before, Shaw's aim was to demonstrate the "vanities of philanthropy." This is not so much to miss Shaw's point as to turn it completely upside down. What Shaw is saying is that Doolittle after his escape from Lisson Grove is a much better social being, albeit a less comfortable one, than he was before. Critics have simply overlooked the ironic amusement with which Shaw views the dustman's discomfiture, which he regards as pure gain from the point of view of society.

Shaw seems to have been inspired to create the fable of Doolittle's sudden wealth by Dickens's use of a similar story in one of his novels. In *Our Mutual Friend,* Dickens contrasts two poor men, one a Thames-side water rat named "Rogue" Riderhood, and the other an honest garbage collector, Mr. Boffin, who unexpectedly comes into a large inheritance. Each is treated as an all-black or all-white figure in a popular melodrama. Riderhood, whom Dickens describes bluntly as a piece of "moral sewage," remains unrelievedly villainous throughout, while Boffin, a kind of illiterate Pickwick, is a paragon of benevolence both before he becomes wealthy and after. Shaw's approach is to roll Dickens's pair of poor men into one, and then to show how the man's behavior is a consequence not of his character, but of his situation.

Alfred Doolittle first appears in Wimpole Street in the hypocritical role of virtuous father, rather after the fashion of Engstrand in Ibsen's *Ghosts,* his intention being to blackmail the two men who have taken up Eliza. When Higgins bullies him out of this scheme, he changes his tack and becomes the ingratiating pimp: "Well, the truth is, Ive taken a sort of fancy to you, Governor; and if you want the girl, I'm not so set on having her back home again but that I might be open to an arrangement." This approach fails too. But Doolittle is nothing if not a resourceful rhetorician. He forthwith throws morality to the winds and argues for consideration, in an eloquent flight of philosophical oratory, as an undeserving poor man done out of his natural right to happiness by the narrow-minded prejudices of middle-class morality. (In an unpublished letter to Siegfried Trebitsch, dated May 8, 1914, in the Berg Collection, New York Public Library, Shaw admits that Doolittle in the play analyzes his character with an articulateness more typical of Balzac than of a workingman.) Higgins and Pickering, enchanted, now offer him five pounds, which he accepts after rejecting ten as too likely to entail sobering responsibilities. But alas, the man who shrinks from ten pounds comes into several thousand a year before the play is over and finds his free and easy life at an end. What, then, is the meaning of this fable?

First of all, Doolittle's moral and social attitudes contrast strongly with Eliza's. Eliza yearns above all things to join the respectable lower middle class. Doolittle, finding that his job as garbage collector is too low on the social scale to have any moral standards attached to it, realizes that he already has, in a sense, the prerogatives of a duke, and is loath to rise. He protests that he likes a little "ginger" in his life, "ginger" to his mind being the privilege of beating his female paramours, changing them at will, indulging in periodic drinking bouts, and pursuing life, liberty, and happiness on his own terms. But Shaw, like Carlyle, did not consider personal happiness the end of human existence. Hollow as three-quarters of middle-class morality may be, and damaging to the race on its higher levels, the imposition of minimum standards of decency on Doolittle is clear gain, any standards being better than the impunity he enjoys as a result of his poverty. If we leave his engaging impudence aside, it is a difficult thing to admire a man who wants to sell his daughter, and it is impossible to like a blackmailer. Shaw's aim as a socialist was to abolish the poor as a class on the grounds that such people were dangerous and contemptible. Shaw held it against poverty that it made Doolittle's kind of happiness all too easy. In a Shavian Utopia the Industrial Police would no doubt have bundled Doolittle off to a labor camp with as little compunction as they would a rent-collecting millionaire who took a similar view as to the world's owing him a living. Doolittle's character does not change, but he is as effectively moralized by coming into money as any hooligan athlete who has ever won a world's championship or any hillbilly moonshiner whose land has brought him a fortune in oil royalties. When Higgins, on the occasion of his marriage, asks if he is an honest man or a rogue, his answer is "A little of both, Henry, like the rest of us." Doolittle is, in short, whatever society wants to make of him.

Conventional farce would have ended with Eliza's fiasco at Mrs. Higgins's at-home, conventional romance with her triumph at the ambassador's reception and a love match between her and Higgins. (It is worth noting that when Shaw subtitled his play "A Romance in Five Acts," he was using the word to refer to the transformation of Eliza into a lady, not in the sentimental-erotic sense. Compare his ironic use of the term "tragedy" in connection with *The Doctor's Dilemma*.) But Shaw contended that most ordinary plays became interesting just when the curtain fell. What, he wants to know, will be Galatea's relation to her creator after the transformation has taken place? It was one of his favorite theories that people of high culture appear to savages or even to the average man as cold, selfish, and unfeeling simply because of their inaccessibility to the common emotions and their freedom from ordinary affectionateness or jealousy. The development of Eliza's relation to the professor in the last two acts is meant to illustrate this perception.

Higgins is in many ways a paradoxical being. He is at once a tyrannical bully and a charmer, an impish schoolboy and a flamboyant wooer of souls, a scientist with a wildly extravagant imagination and a man so blind to the nature of his own personality that he thinks of himself as timid, modest, and diffident. Like Caesar in *Caesar and Cleopatra,* he is part god and part brute; but unlike Caesar, he cannot boast that he has "nothing of man" in him. It is this manliness, which takes the form of obtuseness to the feelings of others, that leads to his first comeuppance. (Page 82 of the typescript in the Hanley Collection, University of Texas, has the following cancelled speech by Mrs. Higgins: "I have tried to make Eliza understand that this kind of stupidity is part of what people call manliness. I did my best to persuade her at the same time, that you, Henry, are not quite incapable of feeling; but I dont think I should have convinced her if you hadnt fortunately parted from her with some words which betrayed some sort of sensibility on your part.") He and Pickering alike have both failed to grasp the fact that Eliza's heroic efforts to improve herself have not been based merely on a desire to rise in the world, and still less on any desire for perfection for its own sake, but are first of all the result of a doglike devotion to two masters who have taken trouble over her. When the men fail to pet and admire her after her triumph, her thwarted feelings turn to rage, and, desperate to provoke an emotional response from Higgins, she needles him so she may enjoy the spectacle of a god in a vulgar human fury.

Yet however much her spitfire vehemence may put us in mind of the street girl, the Eliza of this scene is far from the original Eliza of Covent Garden. There is a new dignity and even calculation in her emotional outburst. She has now mastered more than the pronunciation of the educated classes. When she meets Higgins at his mother's the next morning she is a model of poised reserve, even cuttingly cold in manner. Obviously her old commonness has forsaken her at the very moment that the experiment has ended and she must find her way independently in life. Nevertheless, Eliza's development, marked though it is, is limited in one important respect. She never gets past the stage of judging the world wholly in relation to herself. In this respect she remains a typical petite bourgeoise, who, as Higgins puts it, sees life and personal relations in commercial terms. She has nothing of the impersonality of the world-betterer, nothing of Higgins's scientific passion for reform. (In another cancelled passage, on page 72 of the Hanley Collection typescript, Mrs. Higgins calls Henry selfish, to which he retorts, "O very well, very well, very well. Have it your own way. I have devoted my life to the regeneration of the human race through the most difficult science in the world; and then I am told I am selfish. Go on. Go on.") Once again, as with *Caesar and Cleopatra,* it is a case of the superhuman face to face with the all-too-human. Higgins tells Eliza he cares "for life, for humanity," and her objection is that he does not care personally for *her.* On hearing that she is going to marry Freddy, Clara's amiable but brainless brother, Higgins objects—"Can he make anything of you?" He is chagrined at seeing his duchess, so to speak, thrown away. Eliza in her turn finds such a question unintelligible: "I never thought of us making anything of one another; and you never think of anything else. I only want to be natural."

To all but the most inveterate sentimentalist the relation between Eliza and her mentor does not appear to have the makings of a marriage. Higgins lacks not only the personal tenderness Eliza craves but even the tact necessary to avoid hurting her repeatedly. Not that he wants cunning in his treatment of women. He knows, Eliza tells him, "how to twist the heart in a girl." But in the end, Higgins, who has devoted his life "to the regeneration of the human race through the most difficult science in the world," does not need a wife any more than Plato, or Swift, or Nietzsche, or Tolstoy did. Indeed, Tolstoy's marriage, a real-life instance of the world-betterer married to a flesh-and-blood woman, had a good deal of the same tragicomic conflict in it. Higgins explains to Eliza that he has grown accustomed to her face and voice and that he likes them as he likes his furniture, but he makes it brutally clear that he can also get on without them and that he does not really need her. Knowledge of these facts does not endear him to Eliza, who infinitely prefers Freddy's simple-hearted homage. As Shaw tells us in his prose sequel to the play, "Galatea never does quite like Pygmalion: his relation to her is too godlike to be altogether agreeable." Eliza is not yearning after godhead; she likes Freddy Eynsford Hill.

The central theme of *Pygmalion* is the contrast between the Promethean passion for improving the race and the ordinary human desire for the comforts and consolations of the domestic hearth. The history of Shaw's struggle to keep this dramatic conception from being travestied in productions is in itself a long-drawn-out comedy. The first published text of the play ended with Higgins giving Eliza a string of items to shop for, including a ham and some ties; when she retorts, "Buy them yourself," he merely jingles his change in his pocket, "highly self-satisfied" at the new independent spirit she is showing. Beerbohm Tree, the original English Higgins, neatly subverted this Miller-of-Dee ending in the 1914 production:

> I had particularly coached him at the last rehearsal in the concluding lines, making him occupy himself affectionately with his mother, & throw Eliza the commission to buy the ham &c, over his shoulder. The last thing I saw as I left the house was Higgins shoving his mother rudely out of his way and wooing Eliza with appeals to buy a ham for his lonely home like a bereaved Romeo.

When Gabriel Pascal undertook to make a movie of the play in 1938, Shaw once more found he had a problem on his hands. To begin with, Pascal, in casting the part of Higgins, chose not the kind of crusty character actor Shaw wanted, but the dashingly handsome and debonair matinee idol, Leslie Howard, which led Shaw to protest, "It is amazing how hopelessly wrong Leslie is," and to add that the audience would all want him to marry Eliza, "which is just what I don't want." Shaw's own personal suggestion for the movie ending was a shot of Freddy and Eliza in their new flower and fruit shop, selling grapes. This is not, of course, the way the film actually ends. In the movie, Eliza creeps back to the laboratory after her spat with Higgins, finds him alone, and hears him ask for his slippers.

Critics who argue for a romantic reading of the play, and who dismiss Eliza's marriage to Freddy in the prose sequel as a mere piece of perversity on Shaw's part, have used what they have considered to be Shaw's condoning of this conclusion to bolster their interpretations. Donald Costello, in his meticulous comparison of the play and the film, wonders what kind of "hypnotic powers" Pascal and Howard used over Shaw to get him to accept it in lieu of his own proposal. But it is clear from Mrs. Pascal's account of the matter that Pascal did not get Shaw's approval at all:

> Pascal's answer to the additional scene in the flower shop with Freddy as Eliza's husband was silence.
>
> But at the sneak preview of *Pygmalion* a very nervous Pascal was tightly holding Mrs. Charlotte Shaw's hand. Mrs. Shaw and Pascal were great friends. Beside them, the white beard of Bernard Shaw seemed to be fluorescent in the darkness. Pascal was sure enough that the white beard would soon be ruffled with anger. Eliza was *not* going to marry Freddy, and there was not going to be a flower shop. Instead the rebellious Galatea-Eliza would return to her maker, Pygmalion, with the soft and humble words:
>
> "I washed my face and hands before I came, I did."
>
> And the love-stricken Higgins, finding his old upper hand fast, instead of running to her would turn his chair with his back toward Eliza and, leaning back, he would push his hat up as if it were the crown of a newly anointed king, and say:
>
> "Confound it, Eliza—where the devil are my slippers?"
>
> When the lights went on, Shaw didn't say a word. But there was a faint smile above the white beard.

Evidently Pascal presented Shaw with a *fait accompli* he was powerless to undo. What did he think of Pascal's intimation that Eliza would devote herself happily to a lifetime of slipper fetching? The best answer to this question is the speech on the subject (omitted in the movie) which Shaw gives Higgins in the play:

> I dont and wont trade in affection. You can call me a brute because you couldnt buy a claim on me by fetching my slip-

> pers and finding my spectacles. You were a fool: I think a woman fetching a man's slippers is a disgusting sight: did I ever fetch your slippers? I think a good deal more of you for throwing them in my face. No use slaving for me and then saying you want to be cared for: who cares for a slave? . . . If you dare to set up your little dog's tricks of fetching and carrying slippers against my creation of a Duchess Eliza, I'll slam the door in your silly face.

With these sentiments ringing in his ear, anyone contemplating Pascal's ending is bound to find it amusingly bathetic.

In the screen version of the play published in 1941, Shaw added a number of scenes he had written for the movie, including the scene at the ambassador's party, but, far from following Pascal, he took pains to reword the final speeches of the play to make it clear that Eliza would marry Freddy. (In the 1914 version, Higgins gives Eliza orders for various household items. She then rebels and the play ends as follows:

> LIZA [*disdainfully*]: Buy them yourself. [*She sweeps out.*]
> MRS. HIGGINS: I'm afraid youve spoiled that girl, Henry. But never mind dear: I'll buy you the tie and gloves.
> HIGGINS [*sunnily*]: Oh, dont bother. She'll buy em all right enough. Good-bye.
> *They kiss. Mrs. Higgins runs out. Higgins, left alone, rattles his cash in his pocket; chuckles; and disports himself in a highly self-satisfied manner.*

In the 1941 screen version, Liza replies to Higgins's request that she buy a ham, a Stilton cheese, number eight gloves, and a new tie in this way:

> LIZA [*disdainfully*]: Number eights are too small for you if you want them lined with lamb's wool. You have three new ties that you have forgotten in the drawer of your washstand. Colonel Pickering prefers double Gloucester to Stilton: and you dont notice the difference. I telephoned Mrs Pearce this morning not to forget the ham. What you are to do without me I cannot imagine. [*She sweeps out.*]
> MRS. HIGGINS: I'm afraid youve spoilt that girl, Henry. I should be uneasy about you and her if she were less fond of Colonel Pickering.
> HIGGINS: Pickering! Nonsense: she's going to marry Freddy.

> Ha ha! Freddy! Freddy!! Ha ha ha ha ha!!!! [*He roars with laughter as the play ends.*]

Shaw reprinted the screen version in the Constable standard edition of his works, where it superseded the earlier stage play.) The well-established tradition of improving on Shaw, however, still continues. Tree and Pascal have now been succeeded by Alan Jay Lerner. In adapting *Pygmalion* to the musical stage, Mr. Lerner has retained the dialogue and business of the movie ending. In the published libretto of *My Fair Lady* he has gone a step further and added some stage directions of his own to Pascal's ending. When Higgins hears Eliza returning to the laboratory, Mr. Lerner comments, "*If he could but let himself, his face would radiate unmistakable relief and joy. If he could but let himself, he would run to her.*" When Eliza reappears, he tells us that there are tears in her eyes: "*She understands.*" How Shaw's ghost would chuckle over this, if he could read it.

Of course such a sentimental curtain ignores the whole meaning of the encounter between the professor and the former flower girl in the final act. When Eliza, piqued at Higgins's brusque treatment, proclaims defiantly, "I can do without you," Higgins, far from being hurt or disappointed, congratulates her quite sincerely and tells her, "I know you can. I told you you could." Her emotional independence he takes as a sign of growing self-respect. He is equally candid in his counterboast about himself, "I can do without anybody. I have my own soul: my own spark of divine fire." For Eliza, the very essence of human relations is mutual caring, for Higgins it is mutual improvement. True enough, the rage the professor rouses in her is the rage of thwarted affection, but her affection is that of an emotionally sensitive pupil, not of an amorous woman. Freddy appeals to her because he is "weak and poor" and considerate, but also because he is young and handsome and sexually to her taste. But above all, she knows Freddy wants and needs her, while Higgins doesn't. Eliza's life is the warm, passionate life of embraces, mutual recriminations, even violence, and her temperament is the volcanic temperament that makes scenes when her feelings are wounded. Higgins can be equally volcanic, but only when professional matters are concerned. His is the cold, superhuman passion for changing the world. Eliza's code is "I'll be nice to you if you'll be nice to me," Higgins's that of the artist-creator to whom human material is raw material only. The insistence that they end as lovebirds shows how popular sentiment will ignore any degree of incompatibility between a man and a woman once it has entertained the pleasant fancy of mating them.

Pygmalion: A Potboiler as Art

Charles A. Berst

Shaw called *Pygmalion* a potboiler, and subtitled it "A Romance." As such, he might well have predicted its popularity. But so many qualities of *Pygmalion* so far transcend such disparagement that the play has special interest as Shavian art at its unpretentious best. The central theme is indeed romantic; but as it evolves, its romance is more social than sexual, and fully as spiritual as social. With unselfconscious ease Shaw has combined pure fancy with a kaleidoscope of mythical associations, and, even more, with a keen social and spiritual sensibility which transmutes a romantic story into a modern myth and touching spiritual parable. Critics have overlooked most of these elements because they tend to approach the play piecemeal, isolating themselves on one strand of argument. Except for a nod in the direction of Cinderella and the mythical Pygmalion, along with a brief concern regarding Eliza's transformation, they have largely failed to come to terms with the real aesthetics of the play, the varied inner tensions which account for its special effects and its artistic success.

Pygmalion unfolds on numerous evocative levels. Most obvious is the imaginative, romantic, dramatic situation, with its lively characters and dialogue, a situation which becomes particularly keen and contentious in the brilliant portrayal of the two principals. Impressed upon this surface action are relatively clear poetic and romantic echoes of the Cinderella fairy tale and the Pygmalion legend. Somewhat more complex, but still immediately intelligible, a social lesson and conscience are projected into

---

From *Bernard Shaw and the Art of Drama*. University of Illinois Press, 1973.

the comedy, first revealing the importance of phonetics in the social structure, and, more profoundly, examining the structure itself in relation to individual worth. Beyond this, Shaw becomes far more poetic and suggestive. He takes the elements of his romantic story, his myths, and his social didacticism, and he subjects them to stress in terms of poetic ambiguities and a spiritual parable. The fairy tale of Cinderella does not in fact complement the classical tale of Pygmalion; rather, one plays against the other most ironically. Further, both are counterpointed by minor but poignant themes of medieval morality and modern melodrama. Concurrently, these myths are subject to vigorous social tests. And finally, most powerfully, the action, settings, lighting, story, comedy, myths, and social commentary all aim at the expression of an archetypal pattern in which a soul awakens to true self-realization. Through successive stages of inspiration, purgation, illumination, despair, and final, brilliant personal fulfillment, Eliza progresses toward self-awareness as a human being. Most simply, hers is a movement from illusion to reality; most grandly, she undergoes a spiritual voyage from darkness to light. Thus romance, social didacticism, myth, and spiritual parable converge upon the play from their different spheres, their tension providing a mutual enrichment. And all the while the dramatic scene, vital in itself, maintains a story light enough to be widely popular.

With typical assertiveness Shaw claims in his preface a didactic purpose of making the public aware of the importance of phoneticians. He gloats over the play's success and leaps to a remarkable, thoroughly Shavian conclusion: "It is so intensely and deliberately didactic, and its subject is esteemed so dry, that I delight in throwing it at the heads of the wiseacres who repeat the parrot cry that art should never be didactic. It goes to prove my contention that art should never be anything else." To make his point Shaw is obviously turning the artistic and entertaining substance of the play topsy-turvy, since phonetics are only incidentally its subject. Clearly, great art *can* be intensely didactic, and didacticism need not imply pedantry. The play does bring phonetics into public view, but more imaginatively than dialectically. The importance of language and its use emerges as a cumulative awareness, arising more from the action than as a net result of Higgins's or Shaw's comments. Our primary attention focuses on the human ramifications of Higgins's experiment rather than on the mechanics themselves, but the phonetician and his work are always on stage, impressing their importance on the action. They convey a "message" in the best sense: to the extent that the audience is convinced by the transformation of Eliza, it may carry away some conviction of the importance of phonetics in society, and of language's essential role in revealing and even in forming character.

But the phonetic lesson, alive as it may be, is merely a stepping-stone to a more fundamental message beneath the action. The major didactic achievement of the play is its pointed objectification of the hollowness of social distinctions, and its assertion of the importance of the individual personality which such distinctions obscure. If a flower girl can to all appearances be made into a duchess in six months, the only things which distinguish a duchess are inherited social prestige and money, neither of which she has earned. The message is projected with unique clarity, confronting the perennial fairy-tale mentality which attaches some esoteric nobility or virtue to social eminence. Eliza's individual assertiveness is unquenchable, and the play gives insight into social generalities by reflecting a vitalist philosophy more than a socialist one. Not any flower girl can become a lady—only one with the appropriate drive and talents. As Candida was not held down by Burgess, Eliza is not held down by Doolittle. Clara, conversely, is scarcely a lady, but she is limited less by a lack of money than by a lack of intelligence. True gentility ultimately rests upon properly channeled personal genius, and the barriers between classes, though they provide protection for vested social interests, are vulnerable to the assault of hard work, common sense, and ability.

The didacticism of *Pygmalion* is thus important primarily as it informs the action, providing a ballast of social observation and giving further dimension to the characters. By themselves, the didactic message regarding phonetics may be interesting and the social didacticism may be true, but the phonetic lesson is scarcely world-shaking and the social implications are rather obvious. More influential in the total effect of the play are levels of myth which counterbalance and enhance its prosaic concerns. Shaw uses these imaginative levels richly and suggestively. In contrast to the coherent bones of the plot, which bear a striking resemblance in detail, arrangement, and social application to the sketch of the poor girl in chapter 87 of Smollett's *Peregrine Pickle,* the play's mythical overtones are impressionistic and are evoked by association and selection keyed to suit the dramatic context, not by any strict ordering.

Ever present is the classical myth of Pygmalion, with its idealism, magic, and sense of vital fulfillment. In Ovid's version Pygmalion, repelled by the faults of mortal women, resolves to live single. Yet he so desires a feminine ideal that he sculptures an incomparably beautiful maiden in ivory, whereupon he attires the statue in gay garments and adorns it with jewelry. Without breath, however, the beauty is incomplete and the ideal not fully realized; so he prays to the gods, and Venus instills life into his creation. The ivory maiden suddenly gains vision, and she sees the daylight and Pygmalion at once. Pygmalion's desires are thus fulfilled, and he is united in marriage with his living ideal. A spiritual substratum beneath this tale is not difficult to discern. It appeals to the most basic yearnings of all who are to some degree disillusioned by the grossness of humanity and seek an ideal, one which might be simulated in earthly terms but which ultimately may be found only through the breath of spirit, the gift of deity.

The play offers a close parallel to this appealing level, and the associations of the myth instill a sense of magic into the play's action. But just as interesting are the points at which the two deviate. Like Pygmalion, Higgins harbors a degree of misogyny and seeks to create an ideal in Eliza. Though he is an artist in his sense of dedication, he is a cerebral one, quite Shavian, and his final proposed union is intellectual, not physical. Parallel to the legend, he creates his ivory statue by act 3, decking it in fashionable clothes and jewels, and the god of Eliza's psyche (urged, in part, by Venus) breathes life into it by act 4, giving her sudden, clear vision of her Pygmalion. However, the creator and the created are out of tune, one existing in a world of intellectual austerity, the other inhaling a vibrant sense of being and seeking emotional fulfillment. The attraction of opposites is held in suspension by the stubborn independence of each, and the play ends in tension, not in resolution.

Contrapuntal to the classical, mythical, and spiritual tones of the Pygmalion legend are the folktale, fairy-tale, fanciful associations of Cinderella. The ragged, dirty, mistreated but beautiful waif who is suddenly, magically elevated to high society is common to both the play and the story. A cruel stepmother, a coach, a midnight hour of reckoning, slippers, and a desperate deserted gentleman are integral details of both plots and provide both with the exuberance of romance. There is even a doubling of the "test" in the play, as in Perrault's original version of the tale.

But again, although *Pygmalion* absorbs much of the romantic nimbus, it converts the legend to its own artistic ends. The incidents are jumbled chronologically, reapportioned, changed in context, and they involve variant emotions and significance. The golden coach is the taxi of act 1 which Eliza hires in personal defiance of poverty and in assertion of her rights as a human being. The cruel stepmother is both Doolittle's mistress and, as suggested by Higgins, a monsterized Mrs. Pearce. The slippers are Higgins's, and as Cinderella's fortunes turn upon hers, these become the symbol of Eliza's break with the past, objectifying her rejection of Cinderella notions. The magic of the fairy godmother in *Pygmalion* is social and psychological, having little to do with dress and fine jewels, and the mystery of the fairy godmother is not that of a magic wand but of her collective nature: she is something of Higgins, something of Mrs. Pearce, and a great deal of Pickering and Mrs. Higgins. Most important, the key "ball" scene is omitted from the play, because the emphasis here is not on the fairy-tale climax of the triumphant "test"—this has been rendered anticlimactic by act 3—but on the social and personal ramifications of the real world to which Eliza must adjust after the test, not the least troublesome of which is a recalcitrant prince charming.

Thus the "reality" of the play is reflected against the romance of legend and fairy tale, and the ramifications are subtle and telling. But even further, one myth is played off against the other. If we see Eliza as Galatea, we see her much as Higgins does in the first three acts—as a statue, a doll, a creature of his own making. Conversely, viewed as Cinderella (which is her own point of view), she is vitally, personally motivated from the very beginning, and Higgins's conceit and blindness as Pygmalion become obvious. The interplay of these variants, of myth against the story and of myth against myth, redounds subtly to the complexity of the ironies and to the delight of the play.

Less obvious than the classical Pygmalion legend and the Cinderella fairy tale, but nearly as pervasive, is a medieval morality element. Eliza in act 1 is breaking that little Chain of Being which assumes that flower girls do not hire taxis, and the presence of an Old Testament God may be implied in the lightning that flashes as she bumps into Freddy, as well as in the church bells which remind Higgins of charity. The profound morality test comes in act 2. Here Eliza is The Tempted, most notably in terms of innocent Eve—"I'm a good girl, I am"—suffering from the sins of curiosity and ambition, lured on by Satan Higgins. The symbol of the temptation is a chocolate, taken from a bowl of fruit, the implications of which are nearly biblical: here is a sweet from the tree of the knowledge of good and evil, a psychedelic goody leading to semidivine worlds beyond the imagination, offered by a diabolically clever and seductive tempter whose intentions are entirely selfish. The combination of hesitancy and desire in Eliza suggests the contention of the good and evil angels in her simple soul, spirits like those of the moralities, one urging the salvation of retreat, the other urging the damnation of acceptance.

The temptation is also evocative of the Faust legend, first in the medieval sense of Marlowe's *Doctor Faustus,* which is correlative to the moral context of Eve's downfall. In desiring language lessons Eliza seeks the knowledge and power of the upper classes, a presumptuous aim reminiscent of Faustus's similar but more ambitious goal. Eliza's inclination to cross a socially ordained barrier is a winsome parody of Faustus's unholy inclination to cross a divinely ordained barrier. Higgins becomes the artful spirit, the Mephistopheles who has the power to make this possible and who maneuvers through his own self-interest to render the prospect enticing. Eliza forfeits her flower-girl's soul to visions of climbing beyond her station, visions which are fully as profound to her as Faustus's are to him. And her reward is the damnation of acts 4 and 5, when she comes into an awareness that her former values were unreal, that heaven has eluded her, and she cries, "Whats to become of me?" Faustus's final despair is scarcely more poignant.

But once again there is a typically Shavian twist in *Pygmalion.* The fear of Old Testament damnation in act 2 and the despair of the last two acts are overcome by the enlightenment at the end. As opposed to Eve's, Eliza's soul is saved. It is at this point that the context is shifted toward Goethe's Age of Reason *Faust:* there is a salvation in the very search for transcendence above human limitations. The status quo grows brittle as it crystallizes, it does not fulfill the human spirit, and medieval patterns and inhibitions are shattered as Eliza breaks free in an assertion of individual genius and independence. As with Goethe's Faust, truth may be elusive, but the individual who seeks it is ennobled by his search, and it would have been true damnation for Eliza never to have tried. Mephistopheles Higgins may taunt her and work on her emotions in act 5, but she properly recognizes the devil for what he is—"Oh, you a r e a devil"—and in this she reveals her true state of grace.

The play alludes to a form of contemporary mythology as well. From sentimental fiction comes the melodramatic consciousness which Eliza and her father reflect in act 2. From Eliza's point of view, as a poor good girl she is in dire danger of being compromised by a rich, unscrupulous gentleman, a vile seducer. She is a Pamela, upholding her virtue against Squire B.; a Pauline, confronted by an ultimate peril. Thus she remarks to Higgins, "I've heard of girls being drugged by the like of you," and she refuses the unreal lure of gold and diamonds—though perhaps chocolates and taxis are a different matter. Similarly, Doolittle enters as the melodramatic father of a ruined daughter, demanding satisfaction, anticipating the worst, and, in an ironic turn, deflated and disappointed that it has not occurred. In the very presentation of this consciousness Shaw laughs it away, but he makes a point in the process which is integral to his drama. If the audience can laugh at the melodrama of Eliza and at melodrama comically inverted in Doolittle, no doubt it should chuckle at the romance of Cinderella. The exposure of one should illumine the fantasy of the other. Eliza's fears are a reflection of the ignorance of the melodramatic state of mind which treats life in terms of absolutes and reality in terms of fiction.

As the mythology and didacticism provide an imaginative, provocative reference behind the scenes, there is an even deeper level which emerges from the action—that of Eliza's evolving consciousness. Commentators have observed that Eliza gains a soul in acts 4 and 5, but they have failed to delineate adequately the aesthetic and dramatic terms in which it develops. Eliza's soul grows by degrees, not just at the end. Ostensibly, the lessons and example of her numerous mentors provide the basis for growth. These Eliza absorbs in terms of her vitality and talent, her own essential qualities without which the lessons would prove futile and the transformation hopeless. She emerges as a synthesis of her education, her environment, and her special abilities, her incipient genius flowering in the broader horizons which are offered her by the relative sophistication and freedom of the upper classes. But this explanation only partially captures the poignant sense of real evolution which the play conveys. While the Cinderella and Pygmalion stories are tied irrevocably to myth by the magic of their heroines' abrupt transformation, the Eliza story evokes the overtones of a magic metamorphosis but also maintains a sense of reality through closely tracing a pilgrim's progress of the soul. Poetic realism results from the artistic and spiritual integrity with which Eliza follows an archetypal pattern. Shaw presents her spiritual growth act by act in carefully plotted, psychologically sensitive, progressive stages, and he complements these stages with special effects of setting, lighting, and timing. Thus Eliza evolves according to a soundly forceful archetypal poetry, augmented by the graphic powers of a theatrical dimension.

In act 1 the darkness of the night, the rain, and the confusion of the scene reflect the darkness and confusion which envelop Eliza on multiple levels—physical, social, intellectual, and spiritual. Hers is a world of chaos, and she is swept along by it, oblivious to the suggestive portents of the lightning and the church bells. Eliza's ties to her class are apparent in her confrontation with Higgins, and the scene would be spiritually static but for the sudden inspiration of her soul by a few coins. This inspiration is pathetic and partial, but is as much as her consciousness is capable of at the moment. She howls with delight as she examines Higgins's money, which is incidental to him but the door to grand things for her; and with great exuberance and flair she indulges in the extravagance of a taxi, the symbol of a higher order of existence which is suddenly within her grasp.

Eliza enters act 2 voluntarily, her ambition fired by the feeble spark of trivial good fortune. With flower-girl naiveté, she is seeking economic security and social respectability. What she scarcely realizes is that this deliberate step toward such goals sharply objectifies her initial impulse and constitutes a key second stage in a much grander quest, one leading toward spiritual emancipation. Although she is myopic as to ends, her goals seem most glorious to her, and her instincts as to the means are instinctively correct—she must have knowledge. Her immediate fate is appropriately purgatorial. The dimness and strangeness of Higgins's drawing-room laboratory offer a fit otherworldly background, an apt purgatory for a flower girl. The social battering Eliza goes through, the burning of her clothes, and the curious, hot, exotic bath amount to purifying rigors quite necessary to cleanse both soul and body: the soul, of childish notions and conceit; the body, of lice.

By act 3 the body is clean but the soul still has more pretensions than depth. The light and airiness of the setting reflect the minor spiritual illumination of Eliza, which consists of a more sensitive perception of a higher state and some involvement in it. But she has adopted a new mask more than a new character, a mask which only imperfectly conceals lower-class values. In attempting to live up to the mask and in carrying it off her soul has grown, but in not reconciling the show with reality she is amusingly imperfect.

Act 4, significantly, starts at midnight. In the deflation after the party, beset by surrounding gloom, Eliza experiences the dark night of her soul, the despair of isolation and absence of meaning. But in her despair lies self-realization, since it involves an awakening to the disparity between her ambitions and her means. The values of society seem fragile when compared to her affection for Higgins, but both are frustrations when Eliza can see no hope of expressing herself through either. In this awareness her sophistication at last transcends her facade, and the soul which lays bare its realities to Higgins, causing him to lose his temper, is a soul sufficiently integrated with personality to be able to face social realities. Finally, in act 5, the daylight and the gentility of Mrs. Higgins's drawing room appropriately complement Eliza's union with the social order, now on a sophisticated plane of spiritual identification and self-knowledge.

Her powers are certainly enhanced, and her sense of reality has so far advanced that now she is a match for the professor.

Thus Eliza evolves from confusion, ignorance, and illusion to coherence, knowledge, and reality. The inspiration in act 1, the quest and purgation in act 2, the minor illumination in act 3, and the purgation of the falseness in this illumination in act 4 all lead progressively toward the sophisticated unifying of spirit with personality and society in act 5. By tracing an archetypal pattern in these steps, and by richly complementing the pattern with dramatic effects, the play transcends fable on a plane of poetically endowed socio-spiritual parable. The profoundest aesthetic level of *Pygmalion* exists in this parable, which qualifies the play's less serious aspects and serves as a substratum underlying the disparities, conflicts, and incompleteness of the didacticism and the myths. (Curiously, Eliza's development parallels, act by act, the five steps of mystical evolution which Evelyn Underhill explores in her book *Mysticism,* first published a year before *Pygmalion* was produced. Underhill outlines a "composite portrait" of the mystic path, including Awakening, Purgation, Illumination, the Dark Night of the Soul [anguish; a sense of isolation], and Union, all "involving the movement of consciousness from lower to higher levels of reality, the steady remaking of character." Though Shaw's debt may not be directly to Underhill, it is to the tradition and its universal principles, implicitly expressed by the spiritual integrity of Eliza's portrayal. These stages of Eliza's evolution seem to offer as clear an explanation for the play's structure as do the more conventional elements of exposition, complication, catastrophe, and resolution, which prompt Milton Crane to agree with Shaw's estimate of himself as an "old-fashioned playwright.")

Important as they may be, the evolution of Eliza's consciousness, the didacticism, and the myths all are made an integral part of the immediate vivacity of the dramatic scene, serving primarily to give it significance, richness, and depth. Act 1, for example, is no doubt the most openly didactic part of the play in terms of Shaw's avowed intention. Yet it is managed with skillful dramaturgy, and the focus soon falls more upon Eliza than upon phonetics. The setting and the action, the darkness, the after-theater confusion, and Eliza's pathetic scramble for pennies are dramatically essential to provide a brief glimpse of the flower-girl's world so that her later transformation will be the more graphic. When Higgins is brought to Eliza's attention and she wails in fear of arrest, the crowd's observation, sympathetic to the girl, falls upon the professor. Shaw thus adroitly sets up his platform, and Higgins's performance is not unlike that of a sideshow artist, or, as Pickering suggests, a music-hall performer. The audience, along with the crowd, is given a brief illustrated lesson in the skills of a phonetician and in the remarkable role phonetics can play in society. But at the same time a lively human dimension is maintained through Eliza. As Higgins plays at his profession, Eliza is in agony, concerned about arrest, her rights, and her virtue. Thus the plight of the poor is contrasted with the privileges of gentility, gutter slang is contrasted with the king's English, ignorance with knowledge, humanity with science. As the phonetic message is exemplified, the social message is implicit, but both add to rather than diminish the essential human dynamics of the scene. With her cleverness in extracting the maximum return from her violets, her insistence on her virtue, her assertion of the sacredness of her character, and her laughter at being mimicked by Higgins, Shaw reveals in Eliza an ambition, self-respect, pride, and sense of humor which are bound to triumph dramatically over the soapbox he has provided for the phonetician.

Numerous background elements are subliminally suggestive. The churchfront setting, the lightning and thunder at Eliza's collision with Freddy, Higgins's insistence on the divinity of speech, and the bells which remind Higgins of the voice of God all introduce a quizzical suggestion of divine presence, a morality note. But the real light of the scene comes as Eliza, amazed and thrilled with the relative fortune the gentleman has thrown her, audaciously takes her coach toward the strange glories of genteel life in act 2. This action is singularly vital on many levels, since this is Eliza's first minute step toward self-realization. The spontaneity of the moment, while seemingly trivial, reverberates romantically, socially, and spiritually, all at the same time. The structure of the act is so complete that it could stand by itself. The didactic point has been made, climaxed by a Cinderella triumph. However, the momentary triumph will obviously be squashed in terms of a grander pattern, because the life of *Pygmalion* and the ultimate significance of Eliza lie in anticlimax, and that soon follows.

Act 2 provides a lively exposition of character which is in itself an expression of the social problem. At the same time it maintains a tension between ignorance and knowledge, illusion and reality, fairyland and fact, which renders the scene a fanciful, whimsical one, wavering between humor and pathos. These incongruous elements are manifest in the different perspectives regarding Eliza. To herself Eliza is a virtuous young woman with worldly intelligence, dignity, and great expectations. To Higgins she is personally "baggage" and professionally a phonetic experiment. To Pickering she is a naive young woman with feelings, and due the courtesy one displays toward anything feminine; to Mrs. Pearce she is poor, underprivileged, ignorant, and common, yet a human being; to her father she is little more than the present opportunity for a good time which some quick extortion money will buy. As such views are in constant counterpoint, they provide a vibrant energy to Eliza's portrayal.

Eliza arrives in a Cinderella illusion, a taxi serving as her golden coach, an ostrich-feather hat and a shoddy coat serving as the garb of a fine lady. Her concepts of gentility are founded in the ignorance of her class, and they cling to easily observable surface elements—manners, money, and speech. With these preconceptions and a lower-class shrewdness as to the power of money, she confronts Higgins, obviously to be confounded when he does not fit her stereotype of a gentleman. As he does with her father later, Higgins completely disorients Eliza because she has no realistic context in which to judge him; the scene becomes purgatorial for her as she is reduced from haughtiness to a confusion of terror, weeping, bewilderment, and helplessness. The profane novice is scarcely prepared for *this* sort of initiation into the higher mysteries. She is only equipped to change illusions, from Cinderella to melodrama—she the poor innocent, Higgins the foul villain. It is not until Pickering suggests that she has feelings that Eliza takes up this refrain. She is manifestly incapable of expressing herself or of conceptualizing her state other than in simplistic alternatives, and, in turn, her feelings have shallow definition because she has neither the language in which to express them nor the perspective or experience to objectify them. Thus terror, rebelliousness, dismay, and indignation are all vented by a howl, through which she may reflect different emotions by intonation, but which obscures the expression of her emotion and probably obscures the emotion itself. Eliza is clearly not just a problem of phonetics, but of an entire orientation, and the humor of the scene, resulting from the wide gap in understanding between classes, is also its didactic message.

As Eliza misconstrues her predicament as a seduction peril, Higgins oversimplifies the situation as a fascinating experiment. The Cinderella dreams and Pamela fears have their counterpart in the Pygmalion obsession. By categorizing Eliza as a draggletailed guttersnipe and scarcely allowing that she has feelings, Higgins is dehumanizing her, viewing her with drastically less consideration than Pygmalion granted his ivory. He is indulging in a level of illusion as misguided and potentially more pernicious than hers. He abstracts her humanity in terms of inhuman generalizations. So Higgins becomes a devil in blindness and in method, and the action develops both as an interplay of ignorance with knowledge and of illusion with reality, and as a revelation of two kinds of oversimplification. One involves loss of individuality in dreams and ignorance; the other involves a loss of humanity in taking that ignorance for the person behind it. Eliza ironically lends herself to stereotyping, but Higgins violates his own assumed sophistication in accepting the abstraction. The courteous, considerate voice of Pickering and the prudent voice of Mrs. Pearce, much like the voices of good angels in a morality play, form a counterrefrain to Higgins's demonic, symphonic gust of enthusiasm. But, like the words of most good angels, their admonitions go unheeded.

The grand flourish with which Pygmalion Higgins ends his persuasion is typical of the vibrant associations which echo throughout the act, rendering the complex counterpoint of character, myth, and ideas so effervescent: Higgins begins as Mephistopheles, tempting Eliza with the comforts, riches, and prestige of the world—"If youre good and do whatever youre told, you shall sleep in a proper bedroom, and have lots to eat, and money to buy chocolates and take rides in taxis." He then threatens her with the plight of Cinderella—"If youre naughty and idle you will sleep in the back kitchen among the black beetles, and be walloped by Mrs Pearce with a broomstick"; he suggests the glory of Cinderella and a Happy Ending—"At the end of six months you shall go to Buckingham Palace in a carriage, beautifully dressed"; he evokes shades of Henry VIII, Bluebeard, and melodrama—"If the King finds out youre not a lady, you will be taken by the police to the Tower of London, where your head will be cut off as a warning to other presumptuous flower girls"; he then comes to earth on a pragmatic social level, appealing to Eliza's ambition—"If you are not found out, you shall have a present of seven-and-sixpence to start life with as a lady in a shop"; and at last he concludes with an imposition of personal obligation, plus an implication of spiritual import—"If you refuse this offer you will be a most ungrateful and wicked girl; and the angels will weep for you." The temptation is overwhelming. What chance has a guttersnipe against a professor, the ivory against Pygmalion, Cinderella against her prince, Pamela against Squire B., Eve against Satan, Faust against Mephistopheles, the initiate against the high priest? The devil—paradoxically, a savior—will have her soul.

In the character of Alfred Doolittle, Shaw offers a roguish counterstatement to Eliza's aspirations and reaffirms the potential of a vital personality, even one which has compromised with the status quo. Doolittle has considerable self-knowledge without the sophistication of social advantages. The melodrama which is real to Eliza is meaningless to him, except as he tries to use it for extortion. He is too busy living in the present to lose himself to such middle-class myths as Cinderella. To rise in society is to be trapped by society's inhibitions, and he exudes a preference for the freedom of poverty over the prudence of wealth. Without hypocrisy, Doolittle is willing to face the reality of his sloth and to appreciate the value of money not saved. Yet beneath his frank philosophy there is an element of making a virtue of necessity, and the humor of his candid complacency conceals the pathos of a man who can scarcely afford morals. Everyone may have a price, but the price of the destitute must by necessity be low; refined morality is an upper-class luxury, sustained by adequate bank accounts. Thus Doolittle's rights as a father are worth about five pounds, and the prospect of Eliza entering a "career" as a kept woman is not unpleasing to him—especially when considered in the light of her earlier query: "Whood marry me?" Doolittle has dramatic appeal in his refusal to romanticize his life, and he has comic and thematic soundness in his conscious violation of the bourgeois notions of success which Eliza holds dear. His precipitant rise to the middle classes later in the play offers a comic parallel to Eliza's plight and provides delight as it tests his philosophy, revealing in the same man opposite sides of the problem of charity. As the dependent man turns independent, the social drag becomes society's crutch and develops a new compassion for the middle classes. He becomes trapped, besieged by hungry relatives, and intimidated by money, morality, and prudence. Eliza's success is the sensible man's doom. And ironically Doolittle, so aptly named, is more truly a Cinderella than Eliza, since his rise, unlike hers, comes suddenly, completely, and through no direct effort of his own. The true Cinderella is a freeloader whose success is a fairy-tale perversion of the Horatio Alger ideal. Through Doolittle, the motivation for Eliza's dreams becomes clearer, but the dreams themselves take on an additional tincture of the absurd.

In act 3 myth is tested against reality, with Cinderella acting the part of a lady and Galatea submitting to critical scrutiny. Eliza has survived her preliminary purgation—the flower girl is at least superficially buried—and the bright, genteel, "at-home" setting serves to complement her budding spiritual illumination. But Eliza is thinking more in terms of Cinderella than of soul, and as Galatea she is a social success less in terms of her mythical perfection than because of her critics' stupidity. The disparity between the magic of the myth and the pretensions of the reality, added to the incongruity between the automatism of the mechanical lady-doll and her ill-concealed flower-girl psyche, account for both the humor and the meaning of the scene. Galatea, Cinderella, and Eliza do not mix. The fancily garbed, phonetically molded Galatea is an attempt to freeze Cinderella into an image of beauty and gentility, but the earthiness of Eliza's curbstone background and the vigor of her spirit are not to be confined. Consequently both myths fall apart, cracked by reality. But in her flower-girl ignorance and conceit Eliza does not see this, and in his enthusiasm Pygmalion is blind.

The only clear head in the scene is that of Mrs. Higgins, whose motherly candor and frankness toward her son cut sharply through his bluff and bluster, quietly yet clearly placing him in perspective. Mrs. Higgins quickly grasps the intrinsic reality of Eliza and sees the concomitant "problem," yet in so doing she is as gentle and kindly toward the girl as she is explicit and stern toward Higgins and Pickering. She is as capable of decorously handling the awkward experiment her son has foisted into her drawing room as she is sympathetic and delicate regarding the predicament of Mrs. Eynsford Hill. Personally, Mrs. Higgins is the ideal of candor, good manners, sophistication, and kindliness which are at the heart of true gentility, and, as such, she provides the standard against which Eliza's growth throughout the play may reasonably be measured. Parabolically, she is symbolic of the ultimate toward which Eliza strives, an all-knowing social goddess (or fairy godmother) who puts the large-talking, unmannerly devil in his place as though he were a small boy, and who reveals compassion toward a presumptuous, trespassing sinner.

The problem which Mrs. Higgins senses regarding Eliza is personified by the Eynsford Hills. Mrs. Eynsford Hill is plagued with manners and social pretensions beyond her means. She is a misfit, a social orphan, and her misfortune breeds misfortune, notably in her children. Freddy's good-hearted simplicity might be sustained by a sizeable bank account, but without financial backing he is adrift, socially above entering trade and economically below obtaining the gentleman's education which would qualify him for something better. Clara attempts to become fashionable by adopting the fads and small talk of sophisticated society, but like Eliza, whose colorful talk indicates the wretchedness of a flower-girl's existence, tinting comedy with pathos, Clara reveals through her uncouthness and abruptness the frustration of living impecuniously on the fringes of a moneyed class. Lacking Eliza's natural talents, she is involved in a life of social tag-ends, pathetic in the disparity between her means and her ambitions, and comic in her ignorance of the disparity.

The didacticism regarding phonetics reaches its peak at this point, with Higgins claiming the alteration of a soul through his science. He is only partially correct, and the limitations of phonetics are apparent in his success. Whereas Mrs. Higgins is limited only by her inability to read Henry's patent shorthand postcards, Eliza is limited by her inability to grasp the genteel mode which enables one to walk home instead of taking a taxi and which inhibits one from using such terms as "bloody." As Mrs. Higgins observes, Eliza is a triumph of the art of phonetics and of the dressmaker, but she is *not* a lady. Her acquirements are superficial, and what she has in natural vigor and genius she lacks in restraint, sophistication, and true spiritual coherence. Thus the play pivots on this central act: the phonetic point has been made, and social implications take over; the myths tend to destroy each other, and Eliza's humanity becomes a problem. She has the manners but not the soul.

Act 4 provides the greatest moment of truth for Eliza, revealing her transcendence beyond myth—myth which would, if this were a fairy tale, have rendered the party scene imperative. But any party scene could only display again the illusions of act 3, along with those gains in Eliza's social sophistication which can be better revealed in deeper personal terms here. Shaw delves beyond the point at which most plays would prepare for a rapid conclusion. Prior to this act the primary attention of the characters is on Eliza, her training and her performance. Now that the test is over, the "play" finished, the time comes for plaudits and bows, and while Pickering is generous, Eliza is shoved into the wings by Higgins. The dream has been fulfilled, midnight has tolled for Cinderella, and morning reality is at hand. Eliza's efforts and her importance are denigrated, her ego is shaken, and she awakens to the facts behind her Cinderella illusion. Her despairing cry—"Whats to become of me?"—comes as a true climax to a crescendo of serious concern which has accompanied the comedy through acts 2 and 3, first voiced fretfully by Mrs. Pearce, then more positively by Mrs. Higgins. The cry is reminiscent of Major Barbara's and Saint Joan's, being that of a soul suddenly jolted by an awareness of its abandonment and isolation. Eliza has compensation in her despair, but it is bitter—in the very fact that she awakens to her predicament, she reveals that she has grown up. Her painful self-awareness, the agony of this dark night of her soul, moves the play toward a realization of its deeper social and spiritual implications, elevating Eliza toward the insight of Mrs. Higgins.

Through having Eliza turn this new insight on the professor, Shaw effects a remarkable tour de force which inverts their roles. In act 2 Mrs.

Pearce admonished her, "You dont understand the gentleman." Now it is Higgins who does not understand, and Eliza who finally gains control of the scene with her clear appraisal of the facts. As Higgins managed act 2 on a satanic cerebral plane, Eliza turns act 4 into an emotional purgation, startlingly, though covertly, like a lovers' quarrel, punctuated by the return of a ring. She rejects her flower-girl's myth and her past by throwing the slippers (which in this case the *prince* has lost) at Higgins. To Cinderella the slippers were the means to the happy ending; to Eliza these are symbolic of her social subservience and the falseness of happy endings. Ironically, when this Galatea comes to life, this Pygmalion cannot handle her. Eve foils Satan by recapturing her soul, and while it was Eve who gulped the chocolate in act 2, now it is Satan who literally munches the apple (from the same dessert dish), and there is some indication that he gains new knowledge thereby. Eliza, not having received true feeling or compassion from Higgins, at last eggs him into a rage and basks delighted both by his emotional genuineness and by her control. There is an element of love in her delight at upsetting him, as there is an implied fondness motivating his violent reaction. And finally, though Eliza has rejected the myth, she retains the romance, going down on her knees to search for the ring Higgins has flung into the fireplace, a defunct Cinderella symbolically back among the cinders. But the social barrier has been crossed on a vital level; Eliza has met Higgins on a plane of deeply wounded affection which has strong undertones of the love it overtly denies. Her accomplishment most poignantly reveals her growth.

The soul which buds in acts 3 and 4 comes into full flower in act 5. Eliza has developed from spiritual infancy toward the subtle maturity of Mrs. Higgins, and her gentility is almost an integral part of her personality. She has achieved a true sense of union with society and, in the process, has found considerable spiritual freedom. Eliza's development is manifested in large measure by her coherent ability to realize and express her feelings. The refinements of language and manners and the dignity of being treated as a lady have provided a means through which her intellectual and emotional being can put its discordant jumble of half-thoughts, half-ambitions, and half-feelings into an order that has not only exterior polish but interior subtlety. Her sophistication is evident in her sense of humor, which was so notably lacking in her Cinderella guise: she asks after Higgins's health, and comments on the weather in a sly, cuttingly ironic reflection of her only two subjects in act 3. She is, to all appearances, thoroughly on top of the situation, carrying off her role with a savoir faire cunningly designed to twist Higgins into knots. In the manner of his mother, she now treats the professor as an equal or slightly less than an equal, extolling the value of manners, likening his behavior to hers as a flower girl, and discounting her debt to his science.

Eliza's depth of social perception here effects finely honed didacticism. She is only partly right in observing that "the difference between a lady and a flower girl is not how she behaves, but how she's treated," for clearly the difference between Eliza and her former self has very much to do with how she behaves. But she is now rightly sensitive that it was Pickering and his manners more than Higgins and his phonetics that made a true lady of her. Eliza is riding too high, however, and Shaw, carefully avoiding a fairy tale, undercuts the suave lady with her howl of surprise at Doolittle. From this point on she slips occasionally into solecisms which tie her to her past and make her present personality more whole and convincing. Her snobbery toward her stepmother further reveals that she is not yet fully a Mrs. Higgins. She is too close to her squalid roots to easily adopt the kindness, understanding, and integrity which transcend class distinctions.

Fairy-tale patterns are further violated when the talk turns to love and marriage, with Higgins avoiding direct personal confrontation of the issue by shifting it toward Pickering. Obliquely, the professor dodges. Less obliquely, the woman pursues (though denying it) under the guise of desiring kindness (which Pickering has amply given her), unsure of her feelings and, in striking contrast to her earlier poise, even more unsure of how to express herself. However, such comments as "You can twist the heart in a girl," "What did you do it for if you didnt care for me?" and "Every girl has a right to be loved" are strong hints as to where her disposition lies. (The implications of the dialogue contradict Shaw's comment in his postscript that "Eliza's instinct tells her not to marry Higgins.") Eliza's snobbery and attitudes now being middle class, it seems likely that her affection toward Higgins would seek the middle-class goal of marriage. When she deals in genuine personal terms with him, as opposed to maintaining her social facade, she tends to slip into flower-girl vernacular which suggests the depth of her emotions. Her final declaration of independence would be more convincing were she not to gain such pleasure in provoking Higgins to wrath. She produces Freddy as Higgins's rival in love (Freddy is significant in this context as a vapid, middle-class, surrogate prince charming, primarily useful as a foil); then, vastly more infuriating for a person of Higgins's temperament, she promotes Professor Nepean as Higgins's professional rival. Eliza triumphs in the notion of Higgins striking her. In this outburst he reveals emotional involvement, and even hostile involvement implies a warmth of feeling, a sense of equality, and perhaps jealousy—a reaction which is not scientific, a reality which is not mental. The emphasis of the closing dialogue thus suggests that Eliza may have found financial freedom but not emotional freedom, and Higgins's final request that she order ham and cheese for him takes this into account. Notably, his request involves a contradiction of that independence he has just extolled in her.

Higgins seems to be motivated by a desire for Eliza's companionship, not marriage. He admires her new strength of character as he admires his mother's strength of character, but he values her primarily as she serves his ego and convenience. At the beginning of the act Higgins may have been searching for Eliza with all the desperation of Cinderella's prince, but certainly not with the same disposition. His distraction is scarcely that of Romeo: "But I cant find anything. I dont know what appointments Ive got." Through discovering the unique value of Eliza's soul and feelings, he has progressed beyond the shallowness of his early callous, categorical estimates of her, but he has not learned emotional maturity. Now, devil-like, he tries to keep her for her soul and for his self-satisfaction, little else. Thus Eliza's "Oh, you are a devil."

A close examination of Higgins's character and comments cannot support a romantic conclusion. He is by nature celibate and self-centered, slightly perverse in both respects. His reference to sensual love in terms of thick lips and thick boots reveals a confusion and revulsion which considers marital sensualism gross. And his justification of his social egalitarianism is equally distorted. His statement that he treats all people the same, as in heaven, where there are no third-class carriages, sounds impressive at first. But it seems less noble on the second thought that it provides him with a convenient excuse both for his callousness toward Eliza and for his self-indulgence in a lack of manners. He treats everyone the same, but this is hardly admirable when he behaves as though he were the aristocrat and they all flower girls. Pickering also treats all women the same, but he is more inclined to treat them as duchesses, since he has a sensitive respect for human dignity and feelings. As Higgins's vitality tends to run at right angles to society, Pickering's vitality runs parallel. One is consequently more startling, but the other is no less real. Pickering's charity and kindliness give society a moral meaning which Higgins, with inborn egocentricity, ignores.

Higgins, finally, is a motor bus temperamentally, a Milton mentally, and a confirmed bachelor emotionally—a well-drawn composite which is, all told, a rather formidable nut to crack. He is much like a precocious, headstrong young boy. He requires a mother more than a wife and relishes the idea of an emancipated Eliza being not a woman but a bachelor buddy. In avoiding social trivia he is missing many of the details which, when considered cumulatively, make life endurable and worthwhile; in pursuing scientific truth he is pursuing obscurity, substituting mechanics for intrinsic humanity. His science is tied to the expression of life, but he is inclined to negate life for the expression. Insofar as Eliza brings him to an awareness of his dependency as a human being on other human beings, and to a perception of the limitations of his science, Galatea transforms Pygmalion, and the myth undergoes an ironic extension. But Eliza's success is a limited one, and the chance of a marriage between the two is, for anyone who closely observes act 5, highly improbable. This bachelor is truly confirmed, emotionally unsophisticated, hostile to sentiment. The myths, of course, suggest an opposite conclusion: Pygmalion marries his Galatea, Cinderella marries her prince. Higgins's Oedipus complex might even logically be channeled toward Eliza, since by act 5 she so closely resembles his mother in insight and sophistication. Socially she is now a lady and eligible. But through Higgins's character Shaw counters the romantic expectations of the final act, and he does so with psychological consistency, creating a perverse tension between the anticipated and the actual. Ultimately, only the fairy-tale preconceptions of a sentimental audience can comfortably turn *Pygmalion* into *My Fair Lady.*

The play is thus comprised of divergent elements of character, myth, didacticism, and parable which are mutually enriching. Their interrelationship is in flux, but it is carefully worked to move the drama forward in terms of a metamorphosis founded in reality. Following variant patterns, the play progresses from ignorance to knowledge: the myths fade into the reality, the didacticism turns from phonetics to life, Eliza's spirit evolves from darkness to light. Even the comedy complements a rising sense of temporal and spiritual awareness, moving generally from a humor of confusion toward a humor which seeks order and understanding. Act 1 thrives in chaos, the delight of the sideshow. Act 2 plays levels of comprehension against each other, provoking a humor of misunderstanding, of fact versus fairy tale, of science versus melodrama. Act 3 is Bergsonian, Eliza being comic as she is mechanical, the decorous manner of her presence being sharply incongruous with the earthy matter of her speech. Act 4 involves the humor of a lovers' quarrel, with a comic peripety occurring when the underdog triumphs and the master loses all dignity. And act 5 carries this to greater personal depths through a humor of inversion, involving a psychological and spiritual search in which the total complex is sensitively analyzed. With humor, myth, didacticism, and spiritual evolution thus reflecting dynamically upon one another and incorporated vitally into the vigorous story, *Pygmalion* emerges as an effective synthesis of Shaw's careful dramaturgy, intrinsic fun, and thoughtful aesthetics.

Shakespeare's *The Taming of the Shrew* vs. Shaw's *Pygmalion*: Male Chauvinism vs. Women's Lib?

Lisë Pedersen

Shaw's comparisons of himself to Shakespeare and his frequent, explicit and often extravagant criticisms of Shakespeare are so prominent a part of his critical writings as to be familiar to everyone who knows anything at all about Shaw. Nevertheless, critics have for the most part failed to notice that these same criticisms are often indirectly expressed in Shaw's plays through his handling of characters and situations similar to characters and situations handled in quite different ways by Shakespeare. To be sure, implicit criticisms of *Julius Caesar* and *Antony and Cleopatra* occurring in *Caesar and Cleopatra* have been widely noted and commented upon; indeed, they could hardly have been overlooked since Shaw himself points them out and discusses them under the heading "Better than Shakespeare?" in the preface to his play. In a number of other cases, however, Shaw deals with fictitious characters who, though bearing different names and occurring in different ages, are nevertheless in themselves or in their situations so similar to characters and situations depicted by Shakespeare that it is difficult to believe that Shaw's depiction was not, whether consciously or unconsciously so, suggested by Shakespeare's. In these cases the similarities of depiction establish the relationship between the two plays but the differences in treatment illustrate one or more of the major criticisms which Shaw has elsewhere made of Shakespeare.

Basic to all Shaw's criticisms of Shakespeare is Shaw's belief that the purpose of drama is "to force the public to reconsider its morals" and that Shakespeare, except in the three "problem" comedies and possibly in *Hamlet,* makes no attempt to fulfill this purpose. Quite the contrary, in most of his plays he is content to dramatize a conventional, "reach-me-down," or "readymade" morality instead of working out an original morality as Shaw believed any writer of the "first order in literature" must do. Two plays which illustrate this fundamental difference in the approach of the two playwrights to a similar situation are *The Taming of the Shrew* and *Pygmalion*. Indeed, Shaw's working out of the central situation of the two plays is so diametrically opposed to that of Shakespeare that *Pygmalion* seems deliberately designed to challenge and contradict Shakespeare's handling of this central situation.

The similarities in the two plays are readily apparent. In both plays a man accepts the task of transforming a woman from one kind of person to another, radically different kind. In both plays the man who undertakes this task is an overbearing bully. Petruchio consistently plays the role of a bully in his relationship with Kate, and it is, indeed, the means by which he transforms her from a quarrelsome shrew to a sweet-tempered and obedient wife. Not only does he frustrate her every wish, but he subjects her to mental anguish in the humiliation brought upon her by his attire and behavior at their wedding and to physical abuse in causing her horse to dump her into the mud, in preventing her from sleeping night after night, and in keeping food from her with the declared intention of starving her into submission.

Though Higgins does not resort to physical abuse of Eliza, except for a moment in the last act when he completely loses control of himself as a result of her taunts, he nevertheless does bully Eliza in every other way, ordering her about in a very brusque manner without the slightest concern for her feelings and uttering threats of physical violence which in the early stages of their acquaintance she takes quite seriously. In the act 2 interview in his flat, when Eliza has first come to inquire about taking elocution lessons from Higgins, his treatment of her is extremely rude and abusive. He orders her "*peremptorily*" to sit down, and when she does not do so immediately he repeats the order, "*thundering*" it at her. When she interrupts his speculations about the price she has offered for the lessons, he barks out, "Hold your tongue," and when as a consequence of those speculations and of his rudeness, she begins to cry, he threatens, "Somebody is going to touch you, with a broomstick, if you dont stop snivelling." Immediately upon deciding to undertake the challenge to transform her into a duchess, Higgins begins to issue orders to Mrs. Pearce about giving Eliza a bath, disinfecting her, and burning all her clothes, without consulting Eliza at all, just as though she had nothing to say in the matter, and as Eliza begins to protest he tells Mrs. Pearce, "If she gives you any trouble, wallop her." Pickering's objection to Higgins's rudeness—"Does it occur to you, Higgins, that the girl has some feelings?"—elicits the quite serious reply from Higgins, "Oh no, I dont think so. Not any feelings that we need bother about." Subsequently Higgins adds that Pickering ought to realize from his military experience that there is no use trying to explain matters to Eliza, who is too ignorant to understand any such explanation, and that therefore the proper treatment of her is simply to "Give her her orders: thats enough for her." Furthermore, in act 5 Higgins calls Eliza, among other things, one of the "squashed cabbage leaves of Covent Garden" and a "damned impudent slut," and instead of inviting her to come back to Wimpole Street he orders her to do so: "Get up and come home; and dont be a fool." Thus he demonstrates that his bullying treatment of her has not changed in the course of the play, though she has in that time changed into an entirely different person from what she was at the beginning of the play.

Petruchio and Higgins are alike, then, in being bullies, though they are different in that Higgins does not resort to physical abuse and in that the motivation behind their bullying tactics is different. Petruchio has deliberately adopted such tactics in order to "tame" Kate in the same way that he would tame a falcon, as he reveals in a soliloquy:

> Thus have I politicly begun my reign,
> And 'tis my hope to end successfully.
> My falcon now is sharp and passing empty,
> And till she stoop, she must not be full gorged,
> For then she never looks upon her lure.
> Another way I have to man my haggard,
> To make her come and know her keeper's call,
> That is, to watch her, as we watch these kites
> That bate, and beat, and will not be obedient.

On the other hand, Higgins's bullying treatment of Eliza is merely his natural way of behaving toward people and is not a special behavior adopted in connection with the task of transforming Eliza. On the contrary, as he insists to her, his behavior toward all people is the same:

> The great secret, Eliza, is not having bad manners or good

> manners or any other particular sort of manners, but having the same manner for all human souls.

A number of similarities in the development of the basic plot by the two dramatists are easily discernible. In each case a test is set up to determine the success of the transformation of the woman in question: in Shakespeare's play the test compares Kate's response to an order of her husband's with the responses of Bianca and the Widow to similar orders of their husbands, and in Shaw's play the test involves passing Eliza off as a duchess at an ambassador's garden party. In each case there is a wager on the outcome of the test. And in each case the transformation of the woman succeeds beyond anyone's expectations and she passes the test with ease.

There is even a parallel in subordinate figures between Christopher Sly and Alfred Doolittle, both of whom provide an implied commentary on the major plot developments because they undergo transformations of their own in social status and external circumstances, Sly temporarily and Doolittle permanently, but these transformations do not include any real changes in the fundamental character or personality of either. Sly's main concern in life before he comes to think he is a lord has apparently been in sensual indulgence, and this concern continues unabated. Before he becomes convinced that he is a lord, the person who most naturally comes to his mind when he feels the need of someone to substantiate his real identity is "Marian Hacket, the fat ale-wife of Wincot," to whom he owes fourteen pence for sheer ale. After he is convinced that he is a lord, he first calls for "a pot o' th' smallest ale"; then, upon seeing his supposed wife for the first time, he asks her to join him in bed immediately; and when he is denied that request and offered instead the entertainment of a play, he falls asleep during its presentation. Thus, he does not seem to have undergone any fundamental changes in character or personality. Doolittle, too, for all his complaints about the changes his unwelcome prosperity has forced upon him, seems unchanged in manner and speech, and according to Shaw's epilogue "his wit, his dustmanship (which he carried like a banner), and his Nietzschean transcendence of good and evil" continue unchanged. Sly and Doolittle, then, because their transformations are mainly in external circumstances and leave their fundamental characters unchanged, provide contrasting parallels to the leading women of their plays, who do undergo fundamental changes in character and personality.

In examining the differences between Shakespeare's and Shaw's handling of the basic plot of *The Taming of the Shrew* and *Pygmalion,* it is instructive to keep in mind the principal criticisms which Shaw made of *The Taming of the Shrew.* In June 1888, he wrote the *Pall Mall Gazette* a letter signed with a woman's name, Horatia Ribbonson, asking "all men and women who respect one another" to boycott *The Taming of the Shrew;* describing Shakespeare's Petruchio as a "coarse, thick-skinned money hunter, who sets to work to tame his wife exactly as brutal people tame animals or children—that is, by breaking their spirit by domineering cruelty"; and complaining that Katherine's "degrading speech" to Bianca and the Widow to the effect that "thy husband is thy lord, thy life, thy keeper, / Thy head, thy sovereign" might have been acceptable to "an audience of bullies" in "an age when woman was a mere chattel," but should be intolerable to a modern audience. Nine years later Shaw said virtually the same thing in a *Saturday Review* article. Though he praised the realism of the early acts of the play, particularly in the depiction of Petruchio's selfishness and brutality, he complained that Shakespeare was unable to maintain this realism throughout the play and that the last scene is so "disgusting to modern sensibility" that "no man with any decency of feeling can sit it out in the company of a woman without being extremely ashamed of the lord-of-creation moral implied in the wager and the speech put into the woman's own mouth."

The attitudes toward woman—and toward man, for that matter—implicit in these criticisms are reflected in the differences between Shaw's working out of the *Pygmalion* plot and Shakespeare's working out of the plot of *The Taming of the Shrew.* These differences are principally in the methods by which the woman is transformed and in the final attitudes of the man and the woman toward each other.

At first glance it may seem that a comparison of the methods used to transform the women cannot be valid since the qualities requiring transformation were not of the same kind in both cases, Kate's case involving a change of such psychological qualities as temper and temperament and Eliza's involving changes in qualities which seem much more superficial—speech, dress and awareness of the rules of etiquette. It should be noted, however, that although Eliza was not shrewish at the beginning of her play, she was completely lacking in self-control, very quick to take offense, and very bad-tempered in her reaction to offenses, real or imagined, so that a mere change in speech, dress and superficial manners could not have transformed her into a lady. Like Kate, she too had to learn self-control and consideration for others. Once she has successfully made all the changes necessary to transform her into a woman who can pass for a duchess, Eliza herself recognizes that the acquiring of self-restraint was by far the most important of these changes. She speaks slightingly of Higgins's accomplishment in teaching her to speak correctly, maintaining that "it was just like learning to dance in the fashionable way: there was nothing more than that in it," and tells Pickering that her "real education" came from him because he provided her with the example of self-restraint and consideration for others:

> You see it was so very difficult for me with the example of Professor Higgins always before me. I was brought up to be just like him, unable to control myself, and using bad language on the slightest provocation. And I should never have known that ladies and gentlemen didnt behave like that if you hadnt been there.

This speech expresses a direct repudiation of the method by which Shakespeare allows Petruchio to "tame" Kate, because it asserts that the example of bad-tempered, uncontrolled behavior can only bring about behavior of the same kind in the learner, not a change to sweet-tempered reasonableness such as Kate exhibits. Furthermore, as Eliza continues her indirect attack on Higgins's methods through her praise of Pickering's treatment of her, she insists to Pickering that the real beginning of her transformation came with "your calling me Miss Doolittle that day when I first came to Wimpole Street. That was the beginning of self-respect for me." This statement is a criticism of Higgins, who calls her "Eliza" from the first—that is, when he is not calling her "this baggage," "presumptuous insect" or the like—but it also recalls the fact that Petruchio, on first meeting Kate, calls her "Kate," though, except for her sister, her family and acquaintances all call her by the more formal "Katherina" or "Katherine." In addition, Kate herself rebukes Petruchio for calling her "Kate," asserting that "they call me Katherine that do talk of me," whereupon he replies with a speech in which he uses the name "Kate" eleven times in six lines:

> You lie, in faith, for you are called plain Kate,
> And bonny Kate, and sometimes Kate the Curst;
> But Kate, the prettiest Kate in Christendom,
> Kate of Kate-Hall, my superdainty Kate,
> For dainties are all Kates—and therefore, Kate,
> Take this of me, Kate of my consolation:

This perverse insistence on using the familiar, informal name which she has asked him not to use is paralleled by Higgins's reply to Eliza's request that he call her "Miss Doolittle": "I'll see you damned first." Thus, again, Eliza's criticism of Higgins's method of dealing with her is also a criticism of Petruchio's method of dealing with Kate.

Moreover, a repudiation of physical abuse as a means of dominating a woman's spirit is implied by the fact that in *Pygmalion* physical abuse plays no part in transforming Eliza, but instead appears in the play solely as the feeble, ineffectual and unintentional response of Higgins to Eliza's freeing of herself from his domination. When Eliza, realizing that Higgins will never treat her as she wants to be treated and therefore searching desperately for some means by which she can free herself from dependence on him, hits on the idea of becoming an assistant to a teacher of phonetics whom Higgins considers a quack, Higgins lays hands on her to strike her, and is deterred from doing so only by her triumphant nonresistance. Milton Crane construes this loss of self-control on Higgins's part as an indication that "his confusion is complete" and therefore "Galatea has subdued Pygmalion." Thus, instead of being the means to domination, as it is in *The Taming of the Shrew,* in *Pygmalion* the resort to physical abuse is an admission of defeat, a reaction of frustrated rage to the failure to dominate.

In addition to these differences in the method by which the transformation of the woman is achieved, the other major differences in the working out of the plot by the two playwrights are in the final attitudes of the teacher and the learner to one another. Kate's final attitude to Petruchio is shown not only by her instant obedience to him, but also by the speech which Shaw criticized as "degrading," a speech in which she says that in a marriage the husband is the "lord," "king," "governor," "life," "keeper," "head," and "sovereign" of the wife and that the wife owes the husband "such duty as the subject owes the prince," and in which she consequently urges her sisters-in-law to follow her example by placing their hands below their husbands' feet as a token of their willingness to obey their husbands. Eliza's final attitude to Higgins is the direct opposite of Kate's to Petruchio. She exults in having achieved her freedom from his domination:

> Aha! Thats done you, Henry Higgins, it has. Now I dont care that [*snapping her fingers*] for your bullying and your big talk. . . . Oh, when I think of myself crawling under your feet and being trampled on and called names, when all the time I had only to lift up my finger to be as good as you, I could just kick myself.

The reference to her former "crawling" under his feet and "being trampled on" even seems to be a verbal echo of Kate's reference to placing her hand below her husband's foot as a token of her submission to him. Certainly, here, at the conclusion of *Pygmalion,* there is a deliberate repudiation of the idea of male domination of the female which underlies the theme of *The Taming of the Shrew.*

Furthermore, that this repudiation is not simply Eliza's view, but is the view set forth by the play, is suggested by the fact that Higgins shares it. Though he has a habit of expecting that Eliza—and everyone else, for that matter—should automatically fall in with his plans because in his view his plans naturally offer the most proper and sensible course of action open to everyone, Higgins has never consciously desired to make Eliza subservient to him, whereas Petruchio has, of course, expressly declared that the whole purpose of his strange and violent behavior is to make Kate subservient to him. Indeed, Higgins brands the conventionally expected acts of subservience on the part of women toward men as "Commercialism," attempts to buy affection. He tells Eliza:

> I dont and wont trade in affection. You call me a brute because you couldnt buy a claim on me by fetching my slippers and finding my spectacles. You were a fool: I think a woman fetching a man's slippers is a disgusting sight: did I ever fetch your slippers? I think a good deal more of you for throwing them in my face. No use slaving for me and then saying you want to be cared for: who cares for a slave? If you come back, come back for the sake of good fellowship . . . and if you dare to set up your little dog's tricks of fetching and carrying slippers against my creation of a Duchess Eliza, I'll slam the door in your silly face.

And after Eliza has declared her independence of Higgins, he says:

> You damned impudent slut, you! But it's better than snivelling; better than fetching slippers and finding spectacles, isnt it? . . . By George, Eliza, I said I'd make a woman of you; and I have. I like you like this.

At the conclusion of *Pygmalion,* then, both Eliza and Higgins reject the concept of male dominance over women, a concept which is not only supported but actually exalted by the conclusion of *The Taming of the Shrew.*

In supporting this concept in *The Taming of the Shrew* Shakespeare was, of course, supporting the conventional morality of his own day, and in rejecting this concept in *Pygmalion* Shaw was rejecting the conventional morality of his own day and substituting for it an original view of morality. Thus Shaw clearly used his play not only to repudiate the male chauvinism of his day and Shakespeare's and to support women's liberation, a cause for which he was an early pioneer, but also to dramatize a criticism which was fundamental to all Shaw's complaints about Shakespeare and which Shaw had often expressed in very explicit terms in his critical writings—that Shakespeare failed to create and espouse an original morality in opposition to the conventional morality of his time.

Pygmalion: Myth and Anti-Myth in the Plays of Ibsen and Shaw

Errol Durbach

> *London at 11.15 p.m. Torrents of heavy summer rain. Cab whistles blowing frantically in all directions. Pedestrians running for shelter into the portico of St Paul's church (not Wren's cathedral but Inigo Jones's church in Covent Garden vegetable market).*

We are reminded instantly of the classical origins of the Pygmalion myth when the curtain rises on Shaw's play to reveal, miraculously, a Grecian temple within the modern context of costermongers, flower girls, and opera-goers. Indeed, Inigo Jones's Palladian church would seem the perfect milieu for the Ovidian myth of mysterious transformation—even in modern dress—for Shaw's stagecraft is a perfect fusion of the rational and the marvellous, the secular and the divine. Despite a temperament typically embarrassed by ancient notions of divinity, Shaw discovers in the natural phenomenon of a London storm all the portents of supernatural awe. Eliza Doolittle has only to enter and bump into Freddy when "*a blinding flash of lightning, followed instantly by a rattling peal of thunder, orchestrates the incident*"; and as St Paul's anachronistic clock strikes the second quarter, Professor Higgins hears in it "*the voice of God, rebuking him for his Pharisaic want of charity to the poor girl.*" But for all the promise of its mythical ingredients in act 1, the play cannot be seen to recapitulate the specific narrative incidents of the original myth; and although Shaw retains the basic metaphorical idea of a metamorphosis, he empties the process of all its mystery and insists upon the commonplace nature of

From *English Studies in Africa* 21, no. 1 (March 1978).

the transfiguration: "Such transfigurations," he writes in the epilogue, "have been achieved by hundreds of resolutely ambitious young women." And, finally, he deliberately demythologizes the romantic implications of Ovid's tale. The modern Pygmalion does *not* fall in love with and marry the modern Galatea; and Shaw provides a highly unsatisfactory reason for this radical alteration of the traditional myth. Eliza, he says, does not really care for Higgins: "Galatea never does quite like Pygmalion: his relation to her is too godlike to be altogether agreeable."

What is so unsatisfactory about this rationalization is not its frustration of romance—there is, after all, no good reason why Galatea *should* love Pygmalion—but Shaw's eccentric remark that Pygmalion is *godlike,* and therefore inaccessible or disagreeable. This suggests so crucial a misreading of Ovid as to make it almost irrelevant to invoke a classical source for Shaw's play; for what Shaw has failed to keep distinct (in his epilogue, at any rate) is the important difference between the Artist-as-Creator who carves a paradigm of female perfection and the God-as-Creator who transfigures cold stone into living flesh. In Ovid, Pygmalion merely provides the form for Galatea. It is the Goddess, Venus, who blesses her with life—and there is nothing whatever of Venus in Professor Higgins. In the work of the Pre-Raphaelites—Shaw's nineteenth-century predecessors in the treatment of this myth—the distinction between Pygmalion and Venus, Artist and God, remains very clear and unambiguous: there is no embarrassed rationalization of divinity, no attempt to disguise the presence of Venus beneath the trappings of modern scepticism. In his *Earthly Paradise* (1868–70), for instance, William Morris provides an authentic Ovidian account of the metamorphosis; and Edward Burne-Jones depicted the major stages of the myth in a series of four sumptuous paintings which he completed in 1879. In the first, a melancholy Pygmalion turns his back on the external world to contemplate the world of art—the living women outside carefully balanced by the hard sculptural forms in the studio; in the second, he carves Galatea—hard, cold, monumental, and dead in her exquisite beauty; in the third, a gorgeous Botticellian Venus descends in a flutter of doves and a glow of rose-petals to depetrify the marmoreal beauty; and, in the final panel, Pygmalion worships the living woman on his knees. The series would surely have graced Shaw's lovely Pre-Raphaelite setting for the third act—the Morris and Burne-Jones room in Mrs Higgins's Chelsea flat, a pictorial reminder, perhaps, of the last age in which it was still possible for the myth of Pygmalion to flourish. But Shaw's Galatea flings slippers at the head of her Pygmalion; and Shaw's Pygmalion is asexual to the point of having nothing better to offer his Galatea than a strictly celibate form of female bachelorhood in his domestic employ. If Ovid is no feasible source for Shaw's play, then neither, it would seem, is the Brotherhood.

The most notable treatment of the myth in pre-Shavian *drama,* however, is the *Pygmalion and Galatea* which W. S. Gilbert wrote in 1871—a curious blend of sentimental idealism declining sadly into a form of equally sentimental cynicism. What is significant about this piece is not its probable influence on Shaw—he may or may not have known it—but Gilbert's peculiarly Victorian definition of the myth (which Shaw would most certainly have rejected) and his peculiarly post-Romantic definition of the anti-myth (which Shaw would most certainly have deplored). It is a rather nasty little play; but, in a comparative context, it provides an essential bridge between the authentic Classicism of the Pre-Raphaelites and Shaw's demythological view. The basis of the myth in Gilbert's play is, again, the metamorphosis; and in the absence of the embarrassing Goddess, he leaves his Galatea to cope with the difficulty as best she may. In the circumstances she does pretty well:

> I felt my frame pervaded by a glow
> That seemed to thaw my marble into flesh;
> Its cold hard substance throbbed with active life,
> My limbs grew supple, and I moved—I lived!
> Lived in the ecstasy of new-born life!
> Lived in the love of him that fashioned me!
> Lived in a thousand tangled thoughts of hope,
> Love, gratitude—thoughts that resolved themselves
> Into one word, that word, Pygmalion! *(Kneels to him.)*

The Goddess Venus we recognize in this passage as the transforming power of love, which is surely a charming secular explanation of divinity in terms of ordinary human passion—until Galatea, still on her knees, defines the special nature of her love:

> A sense that I am made *by* thee *for* thee;
> That I've no will that is not wholly thine:
> That I've no thought, no hope, no enterprise
> That does not own *thee* as its sovereign;
> That I have life, that I may live for thee,
> That I am thine—

Here she is again—the Victorian domestic paragon, the Angel in the House, the chauvinist definition of ideal womanhood, a piece of property without the shred of a sense of self, on her knees before a sovereign master. One searches, in vain, for a hint of irony in Gilbert's lines. And it is precisely *this* image of the Victorian Galatea that Higgins so vehemently rejects:

> I think a woman fetching a man's slippers is a disgusting sight: did I ever fetch your slippers? I think a good deal more of you for throwing them in my face. No use slaving for me and then saying you want to be cared for: who cares for a slave?

I have the sense, though, that Gilbert's distasteful manipulation of the myth is inherent even in Ovid, and that the Burne-Jones alternative—Pygmalion on his knees before Galatea—is really no more acceptable as a human statement. The Pygmalion of book 10 of the *Metamorphoses* is the model, it seems to me, of the neurotic idealist—the man for whom reality is so unendurable, so imperfect, that he turns towards forms of the imperishable to assuage the human wound. "Disgusted with the faults which in such full measure nature had given the female mind," writes Ovid, "he lived unmarried." Pledged to a life of celibacy, fearful of sex and death, he can love only symbolic images of immutable perfection; and his romantic solution to perishable mortality is to carve a statue "giving it a beauty more perfect than that of any woman ever born. And with his own work he falls in love." There is a crucial turning away from life in the Pygmalion myth, an impossible demand for perfection as the precondition for any human attachment, and a definition of sexual love as that which seeks satisfaction in imperishable and therefore dead forms. The type and the temperament are familiar, even outside the context of the myth; and they express themselves in identical metaphors. Othello, for instance, just before he smothers Desdemona, compares her to "monumental alabaster" (5.2.5)—for the statue is a tangible symbol for the "cunning'st pattern of excelling nature" (5.2.11), pure Neoplatonic form, both dead and deathless, supremely inhuman and therefore supremely desirable. "I'll kill thee," he says, "and love thee after" (5.2.18). What I am suggesting, in other words, is that the Pygmalion myth—the metamorphosis of dead stone into flesh and blood—contains also the germ of its anti-myth: that form of Romantic idealism that stands in danger of changing living flesh into stone. What Pygmalion most desires is a living doll, Hoffmann's Coppelia, or that ghastly automaton with which Cassanova copulates in the closing sequences of Fellini's film. This is the dead end of neurotic Romanticism. If Gilbert's Galatea evades this aspect of the anti-myth, it is only because *she* rather than Pygmalion is the neurotic—the perfect woman unable to tolerate an imperfect world, unable to understand the adulterous implications of her love for an already married Pygmalion, and—above all—terrified of an existence in which all living things must, by their very nature, die. In the closing moments of the play she reverses the process of transfiguration and recedes into the imperishable security of stone.

By far the most impressive gallery of frozen and petrified Galateas in pre-Shavian drama, however, are those women of Ibsen's late plays: Mrs Borkman chilled to the bone in a suffocatingly heated room, Rebekka West draped in the white shroud of her wedding veil, and—above all—the Lady in White who appears in *When We Dead Awaken,* that living allegory of Life sacrificed to an inhuman Art. Realism, here, strains against its own boundaries to create a dramatic symbol of living death, a sculptural form invested with attenuated breath:

> *Her face is pale and drawn, as if it were frozen: her eyelids are lowered, and her eyes seem without sight. Her dress hangs down to her feet in long straight close fitting folds. A large shawl of white crêpe covers her head, arms, and the upper part of her body. She keeps her arms folded over her breast. She carries herself stiffly, and her walk is staid and measured.*

This woman, Irena, is Ibsen's last and most powerful indictment of the idealist, the Artist-as-Creator, who chooses perfection of the work above all else and who, in dissociating this ideal from the passions of life, merely desecrates his art and dehumanizes his living muse—Irena, his model. Professor Rubek, Ibsen's Pygmalion, is the greatest sculptor of his generation; and he has used Irena's naked beauty as the inspiration for his masterwork—the statue of a divine woman awakening from earthbound mortality into a resurrected state of eternal purity and joy. But, terrified of desecrating his sublime artwork by the reality of sexual desire, he has repressed all passion for Irena to a clinical impersonality; and the folly of denying their love for each other, which is the human source of his creativity, recoils upon him as an act of self-destruction. He has wrenched the soul from a living being to create his ideal—and Irena, in "dying," has destroyed his creative capacity for ever. She can no longer inspire. He can no longer sculpt. And while each is indispensable to the other's awakening from the living death, both are powerless to effect the resurrection. A single indictment re-echoes from play to play in Ibsen's versions of the anti-myth—Galatea's cry against Pygmalion's essential lovelessness: Rosmer's freezing of Rebekka's joy, Borkman's murder of

Ella Rentheim's power to love, Rubek's sacrifice of Irena's soul. For if the creative principle which turns stone into flesh in the Ovidian myth is Venus—Goddess of love and erotic desire—then the discreative principle in the anti-myth is the denial of Venus, the flight from sexuality, the sacrifice of human realities to ascetic ideals. Leo Lowenthal in *Literature and the Image of Man* sees Ibsen as the spokesman of a disenchanted nineteenth-century idealism, a critic of moribund values which no longer serve the liberal impulse. Ideals no longer motivate creative acts; they merely conceal their opposites. For when art becomes a defence against life rather than a heightening of it, then the creative justification of the artist merely degenerates into an excuse for human fallibility and weakness. In *When We Dead Awaken,* writes Lowenthal,

> a comparison with the Greek legend might help to point up the character of Rubek, the sculptor. . . . In this tale, inanimate material is released for the development of a human being, but Ibsen's drama displays a reverse process. . . . The egoism of the artist . . . transforms human relations and men themselves into objects to be used for his own purposes; they have value for him only when they serve his ambitions.

There's a faint echo here of Eliza Doolittle's Galatean cry against Higgins—

> Ive won your bet for you, havnt I? Thats enough for you. I don't matter, I suppose. . . . Why didn't you leave me where you picked me out of—in the gutter? You thank God it's all over, and that now you can throw me back again there, do you? . . . Whats to become of me? Whats to become of me?

—and of Higgins's contemptuous retort:

> How the devil do I know whats to become of you? What does it matter what becomes of you?

One fact of which we may be quite certain in finding analogues to Shaw's *Pygmalion* is that he read Ibsen with enthusiasm and intelligence, producing the first major analysis of Ibsen's drama in English: *The Quintessence of Ibsenism*. "Ibsenism," nowadays, has acquired certain extremely pejorative connotations; and I leave it to others to defend Shaw against charges of reducing Ibsen to a shrill propagandist. But if "Ibsenism" may be stretched slightly to imply a severe indictment of death-dealing idealism, the neurotic Romantics and the transcendentalists, then it is not surprising that Shaw should have found in Ibsen a spokesman for his own ideas about the moral and spiritual values of his society. *Pygmalion,* I think, is a very Ibsenian play—not merely a charming comedy of manners, but more importantly a comedy of morals and the spiritual life; and I'd like to look briefly at Professor Higgins as a Pygmalion-idealist figure who probably has more in common with the spirit of positive Ibsenism than he does with his Ovidian prototype.

Teaching the play, I often find that students develop a strong antipathy to Higgins and tend to see him as another Rubek: selfish, vain, sexually ascetic, and (taking the cue from Shaw's description of him) *"violently interested in everything that can be studied as a scientific subject, and careless about himself and other people, including their feelings."* True enough, he embodies much of the negative spirit of Pygmalion: a ruthless professionalism in which doing something superlatively well in the interest of his art takes precedence over all human considerations, a sexlessness which prompts his contemptuous dismissal of all women (except his mother) as idiots, and an obsession with the creation of empty social forms. This Pygmalion may not carve ideal beauty out of stone, but he does fashion ladies out of the crushed cabbage-leaves of Covent Garden and duchesses out of draggle-tailed guttersnipes—which is to say that the Phonetician-as-Artist is essentially concerned with the metamorphosis of social classes, with the transfiguration of working-class caterpillars into aristocratic butterflies. In this, of course, he is miraculously successful—with one important reservation. Galatea's sculptor, as I've suggested, is *not* godlike. He may provide the form, call it what you will—princess, duchess, consort—but mere form, like the statue, is shape without substance, a social role without those qualities of soul that make it live. Act 3 is a glorious comic exposé of the myth, in which an exquisitely dressed Eliza, every inch a lady of the middle classes, reveals the grotesque disparity between social form and spiritual content. She discourses in elegant tones on horrendously inelegant topics:

> My aunt died of influenza: so they said. . . . But it's my belief they done the old woman in. . . . Why should she die of influenza? She come through diphtheria right enough the year before. I saw her with my own eyes. Fairly blue with it, she was. They all thought she was dead; but my father he kept ladling gin down her throat till she came to so sudden that she bit the bowl off the spoon.

Blessed by Venus? Not bloody likely. "She's a triumph of your art and of her dressmaker's," says Mrs Higgins—and in this she is perfectly correct. But she goes even further in her condemnation of the Professor's playing (as she calls it) "with your live doll." For she regards the metamorphosis, the gift of social mobility from the gutter to the middle class, as a foolish disservice to the flower girl which will ultimately disqualify the lady from earning her own living. Pygmalion, in other words, is charged with the creation of a futile and useless thing fit for nothing, as Eliza-Galatea herself laments, but a form of marital prostitution: "I sold flowers. I didnt sell myself. Now you've made a lady of me I'm not fit to sell anything else. I wish youd left me where you found me." Shaw tempts us to read the play as anti-myth, a parable of the indifferent destruction of a working-class girl by educating her and refining her out of her class; and my students, who tend to romanticize the gutter and who scorn middle-class values, inevitably succumb to this fragment of the Shavian argument.

This anti-mythic reading, I imagine, derives in part from faulty syllogistic reasoning. "All socialists are unalterably opposed to an effete aristocracy of duchesses and princesses and consorts; Shaw is a socialist; and therefore he must disapprove deeply of Higgins's brand of social metamorphosis." Such an argument, however, ignores Shaw's claim in the preface that "the reformer we need most today is an energetic phonetic enthusiast: that is why I have made such a one the hero of a popular play." In 1914 this must have sounded unforgivably facetious—as if the reformation of English pronunciation could possibly save England from catastrophe. But there are unmistakable political undertones, in both the preface and the play, to Shaw's idea of the heroic reformer; and I would argue that Higgins-as-Pygmalion is not only an artist and teacher but an idealist of the political life, a reformer of the moral life, and a socialist of the soul. His idealism, indeed, has much in common with those moral-political aspirations of Ibsen's heroes—of Rosmer, for example, whose life's quest it is to free society from its spiritual limitations, "to win over minds and desires. To make men noble all around you—in wider and wider circles." Higgins expresses the idealism behind his own program of social transfiguration in very similar Ibsenist terms:

> But you have no idea how frightfully interesting it is to take a human being and change her into a quite different human being by creating a new speech for her. It's filling up the deepest gulf that separates class from class and soul from soul.

This is the most articulate definition of the metamorphosis in Shaw's play, and the process is inextricable from the Ibsenist vision of a revolution of the human spirit. Rosmer, of course, can effect this revolution only by destroying all joy in Rebekka, only by requiring proof of her ennoblement in an act of suicide. But Higgins's achievement is *not* anti-mythic; and although he obviously shares the asceticism and the coldness of his prototype (to which he contributes his own peculiar vituperative ill manners), his justification of such behaviour reveals the spiritual socialism that underprops all his actions:

> The great secret, Eliza, is not having bad manners or good manners or any other particular sort of manners, but having the same manner for all human souls: in short, behaving as if you were in Heaven, where there are no third-class carriages, and one soul is as good as another.

An equality of souls in a classless paradise—these are the ideal ends to which a phonetic education is the means. But the gulf between the guttersnipe and the lady is not merely a matter of pronunciation. It is the gulf between the garbage in which poverty cannot afford morality and the moneyed middle class in which morality inhibits the natural depravity of the human animal. "You see," says Higgins, "we're all savages, more or less. We're supposed to be civilized and cultured—to know all about poetry and philosophy and art and science, and so on; but how many of us know even the meanings of these names?" And Shaw, it seems to me, endorses this anti-Romantic vision of society in which savagery and culture, amorality and morality, are constantly opposed. Eliza's transformation from the gutter to the drawingroom is surely her salvation as a social being—not because Shaw despises the working class but because he despises third-class carriages, poverty, the savagery that the gutter breeds, and the moral horror engendered by the dustheap.

The exemplar of gutter-morality in *Pygmalion* is, of course, Alfred Doolittle who is of the dust, dusty; and this play of marvellous transformations traces the double metamorphosis of Eliza from flower girl to princess, and of her father from garbageman to gentleman. The deep economic gulf that separates class from class, in Doolittle's case, is fortuitously filled (as he tells Mrs Higgins) by

> this here blasted three thousand a year that shoves me into the middle class. . . . Intimidated: thats what I am. Broke. Bought up. Happier men than me will call for my dust, and touch me

> for their tip; and I'll look on helpless, and envy them. And thats what your son has brought me to.

Like Eliza, he cries that he's been ruined, tied up and delivered into the hands of middle-class morality, his happiness destroyed forever by enforced upward mobility. Again—echoes of the anti-myth. But those who believe that the pursuit of happiness is an inalienable human right would do well to inquire carefully into Doolittle's definition of the term. As one of the undeserving poor, he lives in squalor with his common-law wife, drinks away his money, and thinks nothing of prostituting his daughter for the price of a Saturday-night spree:

> I'm undeserving; and I mean to go on being undeserving. I like it; and thats the truth. Will you take advantage of a man's nature to do him out of the price of his own daughter what he's brought up and fed and clothed by the sweat of his brow until she's growed big enough to be interesting to you two gentlemen? Is five pounds unreasonable? I put it to you; and I leave it to you.

The politics of poverty are unassailable. But because Shaw finds them irresistible is no argument that he endorses them. The scene may be funny, but it's morally foul. Alfred Doolittle, transfigured into a gentleman of means and lecturer for the Moral Reform World League, may not be a happy man—but happiness, after all, is not one of Shaw's primary values when its corollary is poverty and the moral savagery that it promotes. Doolittle's first gesture as a victim of the middle classes is to marry the woman with whom he's been living, however reluctantly, and undertake the support of his daughter. The transformation may be painful, but a sentimental hankering after the amoral happiness of the dust-heap must be balanced against the life of moral responsibility and self-respect. This is what Higgins must persuade Eliza to understand:

> If you cant stand the coldness of my sort of life, and the strain of it, go back to the gutter. Work til youre more a brute than a human being; and then cuddle and squabble and drink til you fall asleep. Oh, it's a fine life, the life of the gutter.

If money can close the gulf between class and class, between savagery and morality, and change one species of human being into another, then what force is it that can close the gulf between soul and soul to create a *spiritual* democracy? It is this mystery that lies at the heart of the myth—the force that Ovid calls Venus, and for which the modern temperament must seek more secular analogies. Colonel Pickering has helped to shape the "lady" with the nice manners, and Higgins has created what he disparagingly calls the "artificial duchess" in the hired tiara; but the self-possessed Eliza of act 5 cannot possibly be defined by these empty social forms. She has acquired an identity, a sense of self, quite distinct from the shapes into which her Pygmalion has moulded her; and Higgins acknowledges his error in supposing that her autonomy is still dependent on his will or that all her ideas and words are of his creating. He may be able to turn Eliza on as a phonographic mechanism made to speak correctly, but, as he says, "I cant turn your soul on. Leave me those feelings; and you can take away the voice and the face. They are not you." The essential Galatea, the living soul who asserts her independence of sculptural form, is that most creative and innovative contribution to the myth in modern dress—a reinterpretation of Ovid, and a rejection of W. S. Gilbert's Victorian tableau of the dependent creature whose integrity is subservient to her creator's. In this, it seems to me, *Pygmalion* is a genuinely Ibsenist play in the very best sense of the word. For the English champion of Ibsen could not possibly have read *A Doll's House* without recognizing it, not as a shrill feminist tract, but as the most articulate parable of spiritual transformation in late nineteenth-century drama. The narrative events of Nora's metamorphosis may find no direct parallels in Ovid—but the spirit of the myth is dramatically enacted in the literal transfiguration of a doll into a self-reliant and responsible free spirit. Nora may embody many of the anti-mythic qualities of Rebekka West and the Lady in White; but Ibsen knows that no woman of flesh and blood can possibly be petrified without her willing acquiescence in the process of destruction. Bedecked in her Neapolitan fancy-dress, pirouetting and flattering and tittilating, Nora plays the willing capitulant to the social and sexual roles imposed upon her by male sovereignty; and the difficult recognition of her status as some northern Coppelia turns *A Doll's House* into a tragedy of moral education and spiritual self-discovery—a tragedy, because the death of the doll, the destruction of a secure and macaroon-filled paradise, and the grievous loss of her children are the consequences of accepting freedom and self-respect as the primary conditions of life. The Nora who takes off her fancy-dress, who transfigures herself from doll into woman, is a heroic paradigm of the liberated spirit in Ibsen—the self-creating being who discovers in her own spiritual strength that vivifying force which Ovid called Venus. The God in Ibsen is the God within, just as in Burne-Jones's third panel the ethereal Goddess appears (by chance or design?) as the exact likeness of the living Galatea. Modern existential psychology, no doubt, could translate *Venus* into any number of terms: the authentic self, the autonomous being. But Shaw, eschewing both existentialism and divinity, has his own peculiar pseudo-theological vocabulary in which to express the idea of *Venus*. What in other contexts he refers to as the Life Force, he expresses in this play through Higgins's sense of a self-sufficient integrity: "I can do without anybody. I have my own soul: my own spark of divine fire." Eliza, like Nora, discovers precisely this: a *divine fire* which turns dead form into living flesh by defining herself in the face of a stronger and potentially destructive personality. She emerges from the conflict as a fine and independent Galatea, who has only to accept herself transfigured in order to be free; and, at the end of the play, she rises to the occasion:

> I can do without you: don't think I can't. . . . Oh, when I think of myself crawling under your feet and being trampled on and called names, when all the time I had only to lift my finger to be as good as you, I could just kick myself.

And to this assertion of genuine spiritual democracy, Higgins ecstatically responds: "By George, Eliza, I said I'd make a woman of you; and I have. I like you like this."

In this godlike claim, of course, Higgins is arrogantly in error. He had said no such thing. He had promised to create the lady, the princess, the duchess, the consort—but only Eliza can create the *woman*. The divine prerogative is hers. The cockney feathers of the flower girl, the finery of the doll's dressmaker, and the diamond tiara of the artificial duchess finally yield, like Nora's fancy-dress, to that sunny and self-possessed young woman who will open a flower shop not far from the Victoria and Albert Museum—and who would surely deny that Norwegian housewives are incapable of heroic transfigurations, or that only princesses merit souls.

The Problematic Ending of *Pygmalion*

Arthur Ganz

As Shaw had drawn upon a recollection of the nineties for *Androcles,* so he did for his next play, one of his richest, most theatrically vital creations, *Pygmalion,* which he completed in June of 1912. Writing to Ellen Terry on September 8, 1897, he had told her that he had conceived of a play for Forbes Robertson and Mrs Patrick Campbell "in which he shall be a West End gentleman and she an East End dona in an apron and three orange and red ostrich feathers." The persistence of Shaw's vision over the fifteen years that separate the letter and the play is testified to by the survival, substantially intact, of these details of costume; Shaw specifies a "*coarse apron*" for Eliza in act 1 and "*a hat with three ostrich feathers, orange, sky-blue, and red*" in act 2. That Shaw gave the role of the eighteen-year-old flower girl to Mrs Pat, still beautiful but at forty-eight clearly a mature woman, is further testimony to that persistence; that she made a great success of it is proof of her talent and charm as well as of his shrewd judgement of actors.

Herbert Beerbohm Tree, who created the role of Higgins, was a more problematic figure. Though entirely amiable, Tree was according to Shaw so disorganised and obstructive (Shaw was the producer, but it was Tree's theatre) that twice Shaw threw up his hands in despair and deserted the rehearsals, only to be lured back by the other actors. Shaw insisted that Tree had "no conception" of the "Miltonic professor of phonetics" and wrote of his leading actor, "when he resigned himself to his unnatural task, he set to work to make this disagreeable and incredible person sympathetic in the character of a lover, for which I had left so

---

From *George Bernard Shaw.* Macmillan, 1983.

little room that he was quite baffled until he hit on the happy thought of throwing flowers to Eliza in the very brief interval between the end of the play and the fall of the curtain." It is significant that, whatever other ingenuities Tree may have perpetrated, the one Shaw cites is the attempt to modify, through the effect of stage business, what has always been *Pygmalion*'s most problematic aspect, its ending.

That the play should conclude with the happy union of Higgins and Eliza would seem to be implied by its subtitle, *A Romance in Five Acts,* but at the beginning of the postscript Shaw ignores the love-story element and announces that it is "called a romance because the transfiguration it records seems exceedingly improbable." However, Shaw could hardly have assumed that readers of the play, who come to the subtitle well before they come to the postscript, would take the term "romance" in this sense till he told them to do so. And in fact Shaw continues to send contradictory signals in the postscript itself. He first says that Higgins remains "one of the strongest personal interests" in Eliza's life, particularly as she is sure that no other woman is "likely to supplant her with him"; later Shaw observes that Eliza is characteristically ill-tempered with Higgins and "snaps his head off on the faintest provocation, or on none," telling us a moment after that "She knows that Higgins does not need her, just as her father did not need her" but that "his indifference is deeper than the infatuation of commoner souls." Finally, Shaw claims that though in her fantasy life Eliza would like to drag Higgins "off his pedestal and see him making love like any common man," she does not like him (or Mr Doolittle): "Galatea never does quite like Pygmalion: his relation to her is too godlike to be altogether agreeable."

But what has become an impossible tangle of ambiguous hints and contradictions in the discourse of the postscript is held in perfect artistic stasis at the end of the play as Shaw wrote it. When Eliza, after asserting her independence, announces that she will not see Higgins again, he carelessly tells her to order a ham and Stilton cheese for the household and to buy him ties and gloves. Eliza's reply is intriguing, for she does not reject these tasks: she has already tended to some of them and evades, without refusing, the others. Her final line, "What you are to do without me I cannot imagine," verges on being a confession that she is obliged to stay, just as Higgins's laughter at the prospect of her marrying Freddy may be either amusement at what he considers a ludicrous misalliance or a hilarious and disdainful rejection of the notion that it will actually occur. It is essential that these dubieties remain unresolved, for they are the dramatic analogues to the unresolvable Shavian conflicts that resonate through the play. That these conflicts have to do with familial and sexual matters is obvious enough from the passages quoted above, but they extend beyond these to social concerns as well. Like all of Shaw's great plays, *Pygmalion* deals with both social and personal affairs (granted that the emphasis here is on the latter), and as always the boundary between these areas is less clearly marked than one might expect.

Pygmalion does not at first glance seem like a socialist, much less a Fabian play, but it is. Higgins, who appears to notice little beyond his professional concerns, has noticed—no doubt in deference to the social interests of his author—with regard to flower girls and their like that "a woman of that class looks like a worn out drudge of fifty a year after she's married." Later Higgins explains to his mother that changing Eliza into a different being by "creating a new speech for her" is "filling up the deepest gulf that separates class from class and soul from soul." These remarks, and especially the latter, cast a suggestive light on act 1, which is more than a charmingly imaginative prologue to the story of the "squashed cabbage leaf" passed off as "the Queen of Sheba"; it is a survey of the social, as well as linguistic distance Eliza must traverse from "the gutter" with its "kerbstone English" to the lower classes with their shrewd recognitions of marks of distinctions ("e's a genleman: look at his ba-oots") and latent hostility to the gentry ("You take us for dirt under your feet, dont you?"), to the shabby genteel (Shaw's own class) represented by the Eynsford-Hills, to the comfortable assurance of money and position embodied in Pickering. It is reasonable to suppose that the elimination of such nefarious social distinctions and the gradual—that is, Fabian—evolution of a classless society in which speech patterns are not a barrier is the ultimate aim of Higgins's Universal Alphabet, at least in Shaw's view (after all, the creation of a similar alphabet was the cause to which Shaw left his substantial estate). But the matter, being Shavian, does not end there. Egalitarianism is desirable not only to achieve social justice but for an even higher purpose: so that all shall be intermarriageable, that is, so that the Life Force can select couples from the total gene-pool of the population and thus have the widest latitude in breeding the Superman.

This consideration returns us again to the play's romantic, or in the full Shavian sense, sexual concerns. Eliza's demands, after she has by Higgins's efforts and her will been raised to a higher level of being, may have a metaphorical aspect, but that does not make them any less urgent. And from the point of view of the Life Force, Higgins would seem to be more suitable breeding material than Freddy. However, Higgins is not only a prospective father for Eliza's children, as her "creator," he stands to some extent in a paternal relation to her already. Since Doolittle is her biological progenitor, Eliza has two fathers in the play, neither of whom, Shaw claims at the end of the postscript, she likes. In actuality, Eliza addresses her father cosily as "dad" in the last act and seems quaintly snobbish and jealous of his marrying her stepmother, "that low common woman." Nevertheless, she is glad enough to see the last of him in act 2, for she understands that he has come only to get money out of her new protectors and does not seem to understand, or sympathise with, his originality of character.

Since he has come to sell her for five pounds we pardon Eliza's insensitivity on this point even as we delight in the ingenuity with which Doolittle, one of Shaw's supreme comic creations, manipulates bourgeois sentimentality ("a father's heart, as it were") while seeing through the hypocrisies of "middle-class morality," as in this proto-Brechtian exchange with Pickering, who is shocked at Doolittle's view of his daughter as a commercial property:

> PICKERING: Have you no morals, man?
> DOOLITTLE [*unabashed*]: Cant afford them, Governor. Neither could you if you was as poor as me.

(Doolittle should not be granted too much charm, however; compare the amiability of Stanley Holloway's performance as perpetuated in the film of *My Fair Lady* with the extra acerbity of Wilfred Lawson's characterisation, hinting at genuine coarseness and brutality, in the Pascal film of the play.) But despite his lack of "morals" and his characterisation of himself as "one of the undeserving poor," Doolittle seems cheerfully committed to the work ethic, assuring Higgins that he will spend the five pounds on a spree and will not "live idle" on it (idleness, we recall, is Shaw's bête noire): "I'll have to go to work same as if I'd never had it. It wont pauperize me, you bet."

Perhaps it is this latent respectability, as well as his fear of the workhouse (his assurance that he already has to dye his hair to keep his job evokes Peter Shirley in *Major Barbara*), that makes him vulnerable to the bequest that Higgins partially thrusts upon him. For just as Higgins raises Eliza from the gutter to win a bet, so he elevates her father to make a joke. Not only are the actions parallel but they are neither of them motivated by a personal concern for the recipient. In both cases the result of this "godlike" intervention are difficult to assess. Doolittle is saved from the workhouse, but he has lost his capacity for self-gratification, his "happiness" as he repeatedly says (evidently without having learnt, like Marchbanks, to live without it). Moreover he must now marry his "missus," who—in a delicious comic reversal of conventional romantic suppositions—has, he tells us, "been very low, thinking of the happy days that are no more." For the climax of Doolittle's story, as he goes off resplendently dressed to be married at St George's Hanover Square, is what many audiences have hoped would be the climax of his daughter's. Quite in the manner of an Elizabethan dramatist, Shaw makes the subplot of *Pygmalion* a darkly comic parody of the romantic element latent in the main plot.

In so doing, he achieves at least two artistic aims: he fulfils romantic expectations even as he teases them through the comic transmutation of the "happy" ending, and by having Eliza's fleshly father marry, Shaw—through some magical process of compensation—relieves her spiritual father of the necessity of doing the same. (In this regard, compare the roles Shaw assigns to Jack Tanner and Don Juan.) That this relief should be granted is absolutely crucial to Shaw's instinctive strategy as he reworks the material of the Cinderella myth. Having been a rejected child who grew up to be one of the great public performers of the age, Shaw was deeply attracted to the story of the poor drudge who demonstrated her worthiness by dancing beautifully at the ball. But as the material of the play presented itself to his imagination, a considerable difficulty arose if the Fairy Godfather was to be identical with the Handsome Prince. The fantasy of parental beneficence associated with the former figure was hardly to be casually equated with the dream of erotic fulfilment embodied in the latter. Paradoxically, it is Shaw's sensitivity to these emotional resonances that leads him to modify the "romantic" ending and thus open himself to the accusation of "coldness." A lesser writer would have had no hesitation in blurring these two figures and thus purveying a peculiar, though profoundly desired gratification to his audience.

The attraction between Higgins and Eliza is, nonetheless, very real, the more so, in fact, for being a dangerous one, and Shaw must try to find some dramatically viable reason for thwarting it. He offers a hint in the play, which he later expands. When Mrs Higgins complains that her son never falls in love with anyone under forty-five, he replies, "My idea of a lovable woman is somebody as like you as possible." Shaw explicates this suggestion in the postscript, arguing that for an imaginative boy a mother with wealth, intelligence, grace, dignity, and artistic taste can effect "a disengagement of his affections, his sense of beauty, and his idealism from his specifically sexual impulses." In a post-Freudian age this notion seems somewhat naive (though perhaps not Shaw's contention a moment later that for many people less fortunate in their upbringing "literature, painting, sculpture, music, and affectionate personal relations come as modes of sex if they come at all") and apparently came to appear so to Shaw, who in 1939 described Higgins as "a confirmed old bachelor with a mother-fixation," the latter term suggesting the recognition of a sexual element here. At least as much to the point are Shaw's hints to the readers and performers in the stage directions near the beginning of the play describing Higgins as "*rather like a very impetuous baby*" and noting that "*he coaxes women as a child coaxes its nurse,*" hints that are borne out by Higgins's boyish impetuosity, his self-absorption, and his lack of adult social control. Higgins himself confesses to Pickering, "Ive never been able to feel really grown-up and tremendous, like other chaps," and his mother addresses him and his colleague as, "a pretty pair of babies, playing with your live doll." In so far as Higgins's involvement with his mother is psychologically valid (and whatever Shaw's claims in the postscript the text gives no more than a suggestion), it confirms what is dramatically pervasive in the play: that Higgins is, despite his forcefulness and his "Miltonic" mind, a child playing at being a parent, a boy who has somehow become the father of a mechanical doll.

This view is less denigratory of Higgins than it may at first seem, for the artist/creator is, if not childish, often more in touch with his childhood than the average person (Dickens being only the most obvious example). As a characterisation of Eliza, the doll image is open to the objection that she is more "human" than her mentor. This is, in effect, the point that Eliza herself raises in act 1 ("Oh, youve no feeling heart in you: you dont care for nothing but yourself") and elaborates in acts 4 and 5. Nevertheless, at Mrs Higgins's at-home, the supreme mechanical perfection of Eliza's pronunciation and the programmed rigidity of her conversation about the weather ("The shallow depression in the west of these islands is likely to move slowly in an easterly direction") are, in contrast to the crudeness of her other discourse, the source of some of the richest comedy in the play. They also suggest another submerged myth that rises briefly to the surface here, that of the girl whose beauty infatuates her lover but who is then revealed as an exquisite puppet. (The most familiar artistic embodiments of this material are the ballet of *Coppelia* and act 1 of Offenbach's *Les Contes d'Hoffman*—both derived from E. T. A. Hoffman's *Der Sandmann.*) For a moment Shaw, under the guise of comedy, touches on it as well, for he is sensitive to the masculine fears it embodies: that a woman is a different kind of creature—one without a soul—and to give her love leads to the dangerous possibility of losing one's own.

There is, however, another point of view from which Eliza seems to have too much rather than too little feeling, and that view has its myth as well. Eliza is both alluring and dangerous in her role as a woman, but it is not the only one she plays. Just as Shaw identifies with Higgins in his roles as teacher/parent/creator, so he identifies with Eliza in her role as child and sympathises with the demands she makes. Though Higgins claims, "I have created this thing out of the squashed cabbage leaves of Covent Garden," he makes the mistake, usual in these circumstances, of failing to realise that his creation may rebel. "But the monster," as Eric Bentley notes in discriminating the relevant myth here, "turns against Frankenstein." Despite their obvious dissimilarities, the roots of Shaw's play extend into the same soil, or familial longing and frustration, that nourished Mary Shelley's tale. Her outcast creature, after all, acquired his power of speech—and the monster is extraordinarily eloquent—through observing an ideally affectionate family (the emotive failures, however whimsically presented, of her natural father are significant in accounting for Eliza's attachment to her surrogate one), and he turns finally against his creator when Frankenstein refuses to allow him love, to create for him a mate who will relieve his sense of solitude and rejection. That Higgins is a comic version of the mad scientist ("He's off his chump, he is," says Eliza in act 1 "I dont want no balmies teaching me") should not obscure the fact that he fails terribly, much as his nineteenth-century predecessor did, to recognise the responsibilities of a creator/parent (his attempt to calm his housekeeper's fears about Eliza is a—comic as always—case in point: "You can adopt her, Mrs Pearce: I'm sure a daughter would be a great amusement to you").

But Eliza's childlike request for "a little kindness" and her assurance that she is not making sexual demands ("Thats not the sort of feeling I want from you") are compromised by her insistence to Higgins a moment earlier that "every girl has a right to be loved" and her boast that girls like her "can drag gentlemen down to make love to them easy enough." At the same time Higgins's exalted assurance that he has higher aims than personal affection ("I care for life, for humanity") and his denigration of the fleshly world, or as he calls it "the life of the gutter" ("Work til youre more a brute than a human being; and then cuddle and squabble and drink til you fall asleep") are made doubtful by his obvious jealousy when Eliza discloses Freddy's infatuation with her: "You have no right to encourage him." Shaw deeply sympathises with Eliza as a rejected child even as he is both disquieted and allured by her as a woman. Higgins may be excused from being Eliza's lover on the grounds that he too is a child, but he is also a parent-figure ("Ah-ah-ah-ow-o-o! One would think you was my father"), a "higher" father who rescues his downtrodden child but a dangerously possessive one. Wimpole Street, specified several times during the play as the location of Higgins's establishment, is, for persons with literary interests, best known as the address of another household with a gifted daughter named Elizabeth, who was held in thrall by a perversely jealous father. But Freddy is not adequate in the role of Robert Browning, and in any case Shaw's identification is with both father and daughter in all their tangled relationships. The ending of *Pygmalion* is remarkable not because it is elusive—it could hardly be otherwise—but because it holds in complex balance so much of the richness of the play.

The Playwright's Revenge

Arnold Silver

That in black ink my love may still shine bright.
SHAKESPEARE, Sonnet 65

[In the chapter of *Bernard Shaw—The Darker Side* immediately preceding the essay printed here, Silver first analyzes the original version of *Pygmalion* and then traces the course of Shaw's unhappy (and probably unconsummated) love affair with the woman for whom he had created the play—Stella (Mrs. Patrick) Campbell. Silver describes the awakening of the passion between the married Shaw and the temporarily invalided Mrs. Campbell, its development as it is detailed in their voluminous correspondence, and its bitter ending one day at a hotel in Sandwich. By the time *Pygmalion* was first performed, with Mrs. Campbell in the lead, she had married Major George Frederick Cornwallis-West.]

The opening night of *Pygmalion* brought to a climax the drama of Shaw's romance with Stella Campbell. It also spurred him to conduct a campaign of revenge against her, sometimes openly but more often from behind a literary smoke screen. The most accomplished expression of Shaw's anger was in the 1916 *Heartbreak House,* a work that lies outside the scope of this study. What does concern us here is the completion of the *Pygmalion* story, the strange way in which Shaw harmed his masterpiece by adding a postscript, and then a preface, and finally several new scenes, all of which appear in current editions of the text and have led critics astray. To understand why he was willing to damage the play, it is necessary to review all six chronological acts of his campaign. It forms

From *Bernard Shaw—The Darker Side*. © 1982 by the Board of Trustees of the Leland Stanford Junior University. Stanford University Press, 1982.

a little psychodrama which may be called "The Playwright's Revenge," and of course it stars Bernard Shaw and Stella Campbell.

I

The lengthy postscript to the 1916 edition of *Pygmalion* was the opening salvo in Shaw's campaign. Here he invents an improbable sequel to the play's story and adopts an entirely new attitude toward both Eliza and Higgins. We now learn with some surprise that Eliza gives up her ambition to become a teacher and instead marries the penniless Freddy Hill. After a period of floundering they set up a flower shop with money supplied by Colonel Pickering. The venture is initially a failure because of the young couple's incompetence—Freddy not even knowing the meaning of a bank account—and Eliza repeatedly has to beg Pickering for more money. She who had once passed as a duchess also has to endure "a period of disgrace and despair" while studying at commercial schools alongside of prospective junior clerks. And further humiliating herself, she has to request that Higgins teach her how to write properly. At last, with additional backing from Pickering and Higgins, the shop somehow attains a modest success despite the inefficiency of its youthful owners. Then they apparently start a family although absolutely nothing is said about their children. Instead we are told at the end that Higgins remains one of the most prominent people in Eliza's life and that she spends a good deal of time visiting him, no doubt to relieve the boredom of living with Freddy, who is portrayed as an "ideal errand boy" suitable only for fetching her slippers.

Let us pause to consider this story before proceeding to the postscript's equally changed viewpoint on Higgins. Most noticeable is the constant degrading of Eliza. She is "humbled in the dust" as one phrase puts it; and connecting these words to a central metaphor in *Pygmalion* we can see that whereas the writer of the play transformed the grimy daughter of a dustman into a human flower, the writer of the postscript tries to grind her back into the dust. He now changes Eliza's character in a variety of ways, robs it of essential aspects he had so expertly delineated in the play, and abolishes all of her growth from act 2 onward. Suddenly we are informed that Eliza is "by no means easily teachable!" Suddenly all of her independence of spirit is taken from her. Now she keeps crawling back to beg for favors, and she renounces teaching in deference to the wishes of that same Higgins she had gloriously defied in the play. Suddenly she becomes a very ordinary girl whose only talent lies in exploiting Higgins and Pickering for her material benefit. In sum, the Eliza of the postscript is no longer the Eliza of the play, and Shaw has patched together a dummy figure into which he takes great pleasure in sticking pins. (He also has a few pins left over to stick into Clara Eynsford Hill. Among the many oddities of the postscript is Shaw's long digressive account of Clara—"an utter failure, an ignorant, incompetent, pretentious, unwelcome, penniless, useless little snob"—whose existence Shaw somehow finds saved from futility by her determined reading of the novels of Wells and Galsworthy and a job in a furniture shop. Shaw may have sensed that hostility directed only toward Eliza would have been suspect, and by attacking Clara he ends up with an evenhanded display of misogyny.)

This strange treatment of Eliza is by no means clarified by Shaw's professed reasons for writing the postscript. He wanted, he declared, to prevent audiences from assuming that the play's two principal figures would eventually marry. He wanted to prevent Higgins from acting "like a bereaved Romeo." Yet these intentions did not require Eliza's debasement. Nor did they require her to marry Freddy Hill. Nor did they even require the writing of a postscript at all. A few emphatic sentences in the preface could have made the essential point that Higgins remained a bachelor. Or, better still, they could have preserved the fine ambiguity of the play's ending by insisting on the unpredictability of Eliza's later relations with Higgins. Shaw's stated intentions, in a word, hardly justify the document's contents, and thereby license us to seek other motives for its composition.

These motives are easily found when we regard the postscript biographically. It tells us little about *Pygmalion* apart from confirming Shaw's emotional involvement with the play. And since that involvement included the actress who had inspired the work, the outcome of the romance with Stella Campbell determined the nature of the postscript and probably its very writing. Eliza now serves as a substitute target for Stella, and Shaw uses his potent pen to attack indirectly the woman who had seemingly rejected him as a lover. "I want to hurt you because you hurt me," he had written to her after she had left him alone at the hotel in Sandwich. "Give me anything that is false, malicious, spiteful, little, mean, poisonous or villainous, and I will say it only if it hurts you"; and through the postscript he at last finds a way to take his mean little revenge, spiteful, malicious, and totally false to the letter and the spirit of his great play. Indeed, he was so eager to have Stella read the wounding document that he mailed her an advance copy immediately upon receiving it, along with a hint that her new husband would find it interesting as well. For Shaw had also been using his potent pen to take revenge (as best he could) on his successful rival, and this explains why he now heaps scorn on Freddy Hill and turns him into the chief agent of Eliza's humiliation. In brief, it was Shaw himself rather than Henry Higgins who was acting like a bereaved Romeo—an elderly, jilted, and very angry one.

Apparently Shaw's anger had to be powerful to help him forget his inadequacies as Stella's lover and his own responsibility for the affair's termination. Directed fiercely outward, the anger gave him time to mend his ego and to replace his lost love object with another one, namely, himself. This process had begun immediately after Stella departed from Sandwich, when he then boasted to her, "I tower mountainous to the skies and see a pretty little thing wondering at me." The process continued not only in the postscript's diminution of Eliza but also in its elevation of Higgins from the lowly state in which the play had left him. Higgins's characteristics are not changed, as were Eliza's. Rather, his faults are omitted or else treated indulgently. His selfishness and cruelty now go unmentioned, his bullying is regarded as harmless. He is portrayed as a superior man of "philosophic interests," a trifle eccentric but thoroughly decent. His yearning in the play to be more than a block of wood is now forgotten, as is his confession that he learned things from Eliza. Moreover, the writer of the postscript now defends him for the same sexual immaturity and mother fixation for which the writer of the play had ridiculed him. Higgins is now a "predestinate old bachelor" who has happily effected "a disengagement of his affections, his sense of beauty, and his idealism from his specifically sexual impulses." His cultivated mother, we are told, sets for him a standard against which very few women can compete, and certainly not the now commonplace Eliza. When Shaw recalls words in the play contradicting the new perspective on Higgins, the difficulty is removed by verbal legerdemain:

> The very scrupulousness with which [Higgins] told [Eliza] that day that he had become used to having her there, and dependent on her for all sorts of little services, and that he should miss her if she went away (it would never have occurred to Freddy or the Colonel to say anything of the sort) deepens her inner certainty that she is "no more to him than them slippers"; yet she has a sense, too, that his indifference is deeper than the infatuation of commoner souls.

The final clause was added to a late draft of the postscript, and its specious profundity suggests Shaw's willingness to forget the true profundity of some words he had written at an earlier date: "The worst sin towards our fellow creatures is not to hate them, but to be indifferent to them; that's the essence of inhumanity." Yet despite Higgins's deep indifference, Eliza supposedly remains "immensely interested" in him and even has sexual fantasies of getting him alone on a desert island so that she can "just drag him off his pedestal and see him making love like any common man." Higgins is in fact turned into an exemplary man even while Eliza is being ground into the dust.

In this attempt to repair his own ego under the guise of talking about Higgins, Shaw sadly entangles himself in rationalizations that grow like an octopus's arms. For on the one hand, it now appears that Higgins [read Shaw] is simply "too godlike" for Eliza [read Stella], and that he has "formidable powers of resistance" to her charms. Yet on the other hand, he really was available had she wanted him: she alone was responsible for rejecting him and for marrying a lesser man. But on the third hand, maybe it was just as well since Eliza would have been a very difficult woman to manage; she still "stands up to him so ruthlessly that the Colonel has to ask her from time to time to be kinder to Higgins." But then again, on the fourth hand, the man is at bottom truly indifferent to the woman, and this indifference is somehow to his credit. In fact, on still another hand, the loss can really be viewed as entirely the woman's, and the poor thing will have to content herself with frequent visits to Higgins's house and futile fantasies of seducing him. Thus Shaw consoles his phonetician in far too many ways and then shows himself unconvinced by continuing the attack on Eliza and her husband. His words may formally commend her choice of Freddy Hill, but his contempt for that choice is nonetheless pronounced.

While constructing this elaborate defense for Higgins, Shaw embraces the Higgins element within himself. Yet with unintended irony he embraces the worst side of Higgins and shows the same savage temper and destructiveness for which he had ridiculed the professor in the play. He ignores the best side—the yearning to be more than a block of wood, to be brought to life and to receive love, the willingness to acknowledge his gratitude to Eliza and his need for her. That need for a woman to revivify him had been Shaw's very own, as the letters to Stella fully substantiate. But when she was no longer available he sought to deny that the need had ever existed, and he does this by portraying his surrogate Higgins as commendably indifferent to women and self-sufficient. It had become intolerable for Shaw to face those truths about himself which his love for Stella had encouraged him to express in the play. Equally intolerable was it to accept the play's truth that Higgins had defeated himself. Shaw was enacting, more than he could bear to recognize, the fate of his protagonist who again turns into wood.

That Shaw flinched from those truths he had once perceived is readily intelligible, for they could be safely exhibited only within the fantasy of the play, and only there could he harmonize his love for Stella and his love for his mother. Had he been able to do this in reality, there would have been no pressure to write the play, whose form, as we noted earlier, protected his desires from the threat of their vicarious fulfillment. The very same emotional conflicts that had energized the play were responsible for the difficulties of the actual romance with Stella, and given Shaw's nature the longing for revenge was inevitable. By his nature I refer again to the formula which he himself once offered to Alice Lockett: "Beware. When all the love has gone out of me, I am remorseless: I hurl the truth about like destroying lightning." The destructive impulse is clearly evident in the postscript, and Shaw tries remorselessly to take back the love gift to Stella and to show that Mrs. Higgins could be the only woman in her son's emotional life. But beyond this, what is finally striking about the postscript is its duplication of Shaw's reaction to earlier crises in his relations with women. Allowing for differences of detail, the pattern is much the same as in *An Unsocial Socialist,* which incorporated his response to the unsuccessful romance with Alice, and in *Man and Superman,* which was written in response to the unconsummated marriage to Charlotte. In all three instances Shaw repairs his ego by attacking whoever he fancies had injured it and by intensifying his self-love. Just as Don Juan renounces women and dedicates himself to philosophic pursuits and his mission to enlighten mankind, so too Higgins renounces women and dedicates himself to philosophic interests and his mission to help mankind by reforming the alphabet. Both men escape into intellectuality and a narcissistic self-sufficiency. Both exhibit beneath their proclaimed altruism a disdain for people and a contempt for love. The ominous difference in Shaw's treatment of Trefusis, Don Juan, and Higgins is that the first is made to laugh at his pretensions as a reformer, the second is given an antagonist who can rebut some of his arguments, but the Higgins of the postscript is treated with esteem. Shaw blinds himself to his earlier exposure of the destructiveness in the heart of the world-betterer Higgins. He himself now crawls back up on his pedestal and glares down at the world, stonily.

II

The second act of Shaw's revenge was the writing of a short and unintentionally funny preface for *Pygmalion*. Higgins now has the stage to himself as Eliza, dismissively, is hardly mentioned; and the fun lies in watching Shaw diddle with the spotlight and colored filters so as to make Higgins appear ruddy with virtue. Shaw flatters Higgins even more than in the postscript in an attempt to predispose the reader of the forthcoming play to view Higgins admiringly. After all, Shaw now implies, the professor belongs to a choice group of the most eminent English phoneticians—Alexander J. Ellis, Tito Pagliardini, Henry Sweet, Robert Bridges—and Higgins's portraiture, we are assured, has in it actual touches of character drawn from some of these men. Henry Sweet is discussed at length, and it is implied that Higgins resembles him more than the others and actually uses Sweet's notational system (an alternative to Pitman's shorthand) in penning his own indecipherable postcards. Sweet is presented as a soured genius whose temperament was ruined by lack of recognition from academic circles, and Shaw, waxing indignant, attacks Oxford for its supposed failure to do him justice. Having thus aroused our sympathy for Henry Sweet, Shaw hopes that it will carry over to Henry Higgins, and he declares that his serious purpose in writing the play was to make "the public aware that there are such people as phoneticians, and that they are among the most important people in England at present." Henry Higgins, with his usual braggadocio, would claim no more.

Now Shaw is undoubtedly accurate in naming Sweet as one of his models for Higgins, but he is also accurate in going on to say that the portraiture is only slight and that the adventure with Eliza would have been impossible for someone like Sweet. Yet since that adventure is the very substance of the play, and shows aspects of Higgins's character which Sweet did not possess, the resemblance between the two men is superficial (just as Tanner's had been to Hyndman), and we can learn little about the play's protagonist by receiving information about Henry Sweet. Shaw's effort in the preface is certainly not to throw any bright light on the Higgins of the play but rather to deflect attention both from his faults and from Shaw's once critical attitude toward him. Similarly, Shaw is quite right in contending that the work was "intensely and deliberately didactic," yet there is a wide difference between what he had in mind to say while he was writing the play and what he now declares he meant. In the play, as we have seen, Higgins's obsession with phonetics is correlated with his deficiencies as a human being, and he is anything but a hero. In the preface this viewpoint is reversed, and Shaw asserts that "the reformer England needs today is an energetic phonetic enthusiast: that is why I have made such a one the hero of a popular play."

Heroic Henry Higgins! Even Shaw at his most assertive cannot convince us or himself of such an absurdity, and therefore he emphasizes his hero's vocation rather than his person, hiding the man behind the mission. But in order to do this, he must now make extravagant claims for phonetics and assume as unarguable that changes in the way a language is spelled will vastly improve the way it is pronounced. Shaw had always been interested in phonetics, it is true, and indeed in the play he had simultaneously used his knowledge of the subject and teased himself for overrating its importance. As early as 1890, even while defending phonetics, he had fair-mindedly recognized that "most men become humbugs when they learn elocution" and "that the elocutionary man is the most insufferable of human beings." But now a quarter of a century later, under the compulsion to defend Higgins, he loses his balance and launches his own career as a famous crank on the subject. The very sounds of a crank, the ill-tempered exaggerations and the implied promise of a cure-all, are heard in the preface's opening paragraphs:

> The English have no respect for their language, and will not teach their children to speak it. They cannot spell it because they have nothing to spell it with but an old foreign alphabet of which only the consonants—and not all of them—have any agreed speech value. Consequently no man can teach himself what it should sound like from reading it; and it is impossible for an Englishman to open his mouth without making some other Englishman despise him.

This has the true Higginsian ring, which will hereafter be heard in all of Shaw's declarations as a phonetical missionary out to prove in his own person that Henry Higgins was absolutely right. Even death itself could not stop Shaw from proclaiming the new gospel: in his will he left the bulk of his residuary estate to the furtherance of Higgins's scheme to save the English-speaking world through alphabetical reform, to the "launching, advertising and propaganda" of a new British Alphabet. The lengthy codicils in Shaw's last testament which deal with these matters seem to have been dictated by Henry Higgins himself, and they testify as it were to Shaw's persistence in defending Higgins and in seeking to cancel, even from beyond the grave, the mocking self-exposure that his love for Stella Campbell had once emboldened him to undertake.

III

The next three acts of The Playwright's Revenge were not directly related to *Pygmalion,* but they nonetheless throw light on the play's final revisions. The first of these attacks was incorporated into *Back to Methuselah,* begun in 1918. It is a work which fulfills Shaw's warning to Stella that if she rejected him it would "turn me into rusty iron and cut me off for ever from what is common and young in my humanity," and that he would be able to relieve himself only with "hideous laughter, joyless, hard, dead." The laughter in this huge and misanthropic work is hideous indeed as Shaw sneers at love and youth and at the very method of procreating the human species. But from our present vantage ground we can see him almost giving away the reason for the hideous laughter when he introduces toward the end, in a utopia set twenty thousand years into the future, a little scene involving none other than a scientist named Pygmalion who is trying to create artificial people. Having finally succeeded in his experiments, he now brings forth for their debut two synthetic creatures, a man and woman from the twentieth century, "of noble appearance, beautifully modelled and splendidly attired." Pygmalion rejects an onlooker's contention that his creatures are merely automata. They are, he says, typical humans of a primitive early time, for they lie and they posture and they boast, they are craven and vicious; and during their brief appearance they demonstrate all these traits. "Can they make love?" someone asks. "Yes," Pygmalion replies, "they can respond to every stimulus. They have all the reflexes. Put your arm round the man's neck, and he will put his arm round your body. He cannot help it." "Have they feelings?" "Of course they have," says Pygmalion; "I tell you, they have all the reflexes." But Shaw does not stop with these sardonic comments on the human creatures he has bodied forth, lovely in appearance, repulsive in behavior. He makes the two figures start to fight, and the female picks up a stone to hurl at her consort:

> *Pygmalion, seeing what is happening, hurls himself on the Female Figure and wrenches the stone out of her hand. All spring up in consternation.*

ARJILLAX: She meant to kill him.
STREPHON: This is horrible.
THE FEMALE FIGURE [*wrestling with Pygmalion*]: Let me go. Let me go, will you [*She bites his hand*].
PYGMALION [*releasing her and staggering*]: Oh!
A general shriek of horror echoes his exclamation. He turns deadly pale, and supports himself against the end of the curved seat.
THE FEMALE FIGURE [*to her consort*]: You would stand there and let me be treated like this, you unmanly coward.
Pygmalion falls dead.
THE NEWLY BORN: Oh! Whats the matter? Why did he fall? What has happened to him?
They look on anxiously as Martellus kneels down and examines the body of Pygmalion.
MARTELLUS: She has bitten a piece out of his hand nearly as large as a finger nail: enough to kill ten men. There is no pulse, no breath.

This is one of the few vivid moments of action in an otherwise garrulous play, and an audience would welcome it despite its abrupt touch of horror. Yet what is suggestive about the incident in our present context is how fully Shaw departs from the Pygmalion story in having the life-giver killed by his female creation. Was this, we may wonder, meant to be an exaggerated parable of his own fate in his dealings with Stella? Was it meant to convey to her a private message when she saw the play? Surely in naming a character Pygmalion, Shaw had to have had in mind his famous play of that name and its many associations with Stella. He even is drawn to the imagery of biting which appeared in the confrontation scene in act 4 between Eliza and Higgins, and he now carries that scene's masochistic impulses to their psychological conclusion in Pygmalion's death. We recall too that Eliza's story had first occurred to Shaw when he was writing for Stella the role of Cleopatra, and appropriately enough the female automaton is here called Cleopatra-Semiramis. Eliza had turned against Higgins and hurt him just as Stella was to do to Shaw; now when the woman fatally bites the hand of her creator, Shaw seems to be indicating under a protective cover of fantasy that Stella Campbell had killed something important in him. But he was still surviving well enough, it should immediately be added, to see to it that the character who had destroyed her Pygmalion was then herself killed as well.

IV

Thus far Shaw's chief acts of revenge were literary, and only in fantasy could he obliterate the supposedly ungrateful woman. But now we come to a seriocomic episode in which Stella Campbell tried to strike back. Ever since the opening night of *Pygmalion,* Shaw had been doing what he safely could to hurt her although outwardly they still remained friends. He even acknowledged to her his professional indebtedness for the several characters he had gotten "out of your manifold nature": Cleopatra, Eliza, Mrs. Hushabye, the Serpent. "I exploited you, made money out of you," he admitted. "Why, oh why do you get nothing out of me, though I get everything out of you? . . . You are the Vamp and I the victim; yet it is I who suck your blood and fatten on it whilst you lose everything! It is ridiculous! There's something wrong somewhere." What was wrong, as Mrs. Campbell knew, was that Shaw would do nothing to help her even when the opportunity arose. He ridiculed her behind her back, made her fear that he would advise theatre managers not to employ her, and refused to let her play the role of Mrs. Hushabye in *Heartbreak House* even though she had inspired the character, would have played it brilliantly, and was having difficulty finding parts suitable for an actress now in her mid-fifties. What Mrs. Campbell may not have realized was that she *was* playing a leading role as the victim in the unfolding drama of The Playwright's Revenge, and that Shaw's refusal to let her act in his plays was part of the scenario.

But he was not to have everything his own way. He found that other people too could retaliate verbally, not by fantasizing but simply by telling the truth. Stella, needing money, had begun in 1921 to write her autobiography, and when Shaw learned of this he nervously stretched forth a helping hand. He put at her disposal his professional skill in connecting her "tidbits into dignified paragraphs," he hinted at the need to be circumspect lest she damage her reputation, he advised her with seeming disinterestedness of the legal consequences of publishing letters without the permission of the sender. Her own dignity, he always implied, was uppermost in his mind. Yet he could not always maintain the guise of the serviceable friend, and occasionally his alarm showed through. "If you send me *all* the letters that survive," he suggested to her, betraying his concern by emphasizing the *all,* "it may be possible to work in quite a good deal of them harmlessly and amusingly." Stella teased him for his anxiety, for putting on his "suburban cap," for not realizing that his letters actually did credit to him as a man of feeling. Shaw then reacted angrily and warned her that she would have to "give up the idea of making any use of the letters once and for all." They would offend Charlotte and "make mischief in my household"; they would be construed as showing an "author who tried to seduce you when you were an unprotected widow"; in short, a woman who published "love letters from a married man to a woman who is not his wife . . . is a rotter and a courtesan." Stella refrained from quoting to the self-proclaimed superman the words he had used in an early play to show how a real hero dealt with such matters—the Duke of Wellington's response to a woman who threatened to publish his letters to her: "'Dear Jenny: publish and be damned. Yours affectionately, Wellington.'" Instead, she tried to have her publisher release her from the understanding that she would include Shaw's letters. She also sent Shaw a bundle of letters to examine with Charlotte and make cuts of passages "that could hurt Charlotte." He did not let his wife look at the letters but, seeming to imply that he had done so, sent them back with extensive deletions indicated. Stella responded with the words: "It is a supreme pity that you have massacred the letters as you have done; they are now the only insincere thing in the book." Shaw also corresponded with her publisher to bring pressure on her, and in the end, after further surgery, the book finally appeared. It contained only a few of the most innocuous of the letters along with a handsome tribute to her friend's kindness.

Shaw had won. And the famous scoffer at bourgeois respectability, the dedicated advocate of truth, probably enjoyed his success in the role of the Reverend Bowdler, which he was to play throughout his lifetime with his several biographers and when writing his own reminiscences. Yet he knew that he had won only a temporary victory since the letters still existed, and so for the next eighteen years, until Stella's death in 1940, he continued to refuse her permission to sell or to publish any of them though she was facing actual poverty. His refusals were avowedly based on the desire to protect Charlotte from embarrassment, but that pretense of gallantry was exposed when even after his wife's death he still refused permission. Only after his own death was the correspondence allowed to appear.

V

To prepare the world for that posthumous day, Shaw eventually decided to give his own version of the affair with Stella. As a world-renowned author, and since 1925 a Nobel Laureate, he was exceedingly conscious of his place in history, and more than ever before he wrote with an eye to his future reputation. He advised Stella that "we must not be handed down to history by ignoble gossip and venomous slander" or, he might have added, by the unadorned portrait of himself that would someday appear in their letters. To touch up that portrait, and to take his most direct revenge, he decided in 1929 to amplify his notion of Stella as a courtesan by inserting into the middle of *The Apple Cart,* his next play but one after *Back to Methuselah,* a scene ostensibly drawn from the days of their romance. It was a scene without much relevance to the play, as he himself acknowledged by designating it "An Interlude," but he wrote it anyway because he wanted to influence posterity's judgment of his romance and wanted also the immediate satisfaction of humiliating Stella publicly—he broadcast the fact that she alone was the model for Orinthia, the play's courtesan.

The play as a whole is set in England in the latter twentieth century and deals with a power struggle between King Magnus, a dedicated and urbane ruler, and his Prime Minister. Each of the play's two acts features an argumentative meeting between Magnus and the Cabinet; and in the end he preserves his power by threatening to abdicate and become leader of a new political party. During the interlude between the acts he visits the beautiful Orinthia in her rooms in the palace. She immediately starts a quarrel with him, complains of being neglected, and attacks his Queen Jemima:

> ORINTHIA: Everyone knows that I am the real queen. Everyone treats me as the real queen. They cheer me in the streets. When I open one of the art exhibitions or launch a new ship they crowd the place out. I am one of Nature's queens; and they know it. If you do not, you are not one of Nature's kings.
>
> MAGNUS: Sublime! Nothing but genuine inspiration could give a woman such cheek.
>
> ORINTHIA: Yes: inspiration, not cheek. [*Sitting as before*] Magnus: when are you going to face my destiny, and your own?
>
> MAGNUS: But my wife? the queen? What is to become of my poor dear Jemima?
>
> ORINTHIA: Oh, drown her: shoot her: tell your chauffeur to drive her into the Serpentine and leave her there. The woman makes you ridiculous.

MAGNUS: I dont think I should like that. And the public would think it illnatured.

ORINTHIA: Oh, you know what I mean. Divorce her. Make her divorce you. . . . Everybody does it when they need a change.

MAGNUS: But I cant imagine what I should do without Jemima.

ORINTHIA: Nobody else can imagine what you do with her. But you need not do without her. You can see as much of her as you like when we are married. I shall not be jealous and make scenes.

MAGNUS: That is very magnanimous of you. But I am afraid it does not settle the difficulty. Jemima would not think it right to keep up her present intimacy with me if I were married to you.

ORINTHIA: What a woman!

They continue in the same key, with Shaw giving Orinthia self-damning speeches on a variety of topics. She exhibits vanity and triviality, financial extravagance and mental narrowness. She loathes women who take an interest in politics, and she urges Magnus to be the sort of king who will "wipe [his] boots on common people." When Magnus finally tries to leave to take tea with his wife, Orinthia forcibly restrains him. They struggle on the settee and then she drags him to the floor, where they wrestle with each other until the King's secretary enters and Magnus can effect his escape.

Shaw did all he could do, while treading the edge of the libel laws, to make clear that Orinthia was modeled on Stella Campbell. He toyed with the astral image of her name and made allusions to her autobiography's account of their relationship. He made reference to her two marriages and imputed to her sole responsibility for their failure. He tastelessly alluded to her only son, Alan, who had died in battle in 1918. He also let it be known that the grappling on the floor was based on an incident years earlier at Stella's house, when supposedly she tried to restrain him from rushing back to have a punctual tea with Charlotte. There are of course details that differentiate Stella from Orinthia, and, even more, King Magnus from Shaw; yet the King's relations with Orinthia are manifestly intended to epitomize Shaw's own with Stella. Magnus is portrayed as a well-meaning, patient man, exploited by an exceptionally beautiful siren, but firm in his loyalty to his wife. He defends that wife's workaday value even while justifying his relations with another woman.

The portrait of Stella as Orinthia is suavely devastating. But it is not dramatically convincing. Given Orinthia's inadequacies of mind and character, and her appetite for quarreling, it is hard to credit the King's remarks that she is his "queen in fairyland" and that he goes to see her "to enjoy talking to you like this when I need an hour's respite from royalty: when my stupid wife has been worrying me." Physical beauty is all that Orinthia has to offer, and sexual pleasure is the only imaginable reason for keeping her; yet even while Shaw encourages this supposition he also hints at its negation. Orinthia is apparently resisting Magnus until he marries her:

> MAGNUS: My dear Orinthia, I had rather marry the devil. Being a wife is not your job.
>
> ORINTHIA: You think so because you have no imagination. And you dont know me because I have never let you really possess me. I should make you more happy than any man has ever yet been on earth.
>
> MAGNUS: I defy you to make me more happy than our strangely innocent relations have already made me.
>
> ORINTHIA [*rising restlessly*]: You talk like a child or a saint. [*Turning on him*] I can give you a new life: one of which you have no conception. I can give you beautiful, wonderful children.

Orinthia, we are startled to realize, is kept in the palace and pensioned by the state to serve as a nagging *platonic* mistress. What prompts the King to have such unnatural tastes, and to expend public funds on so sterile an enterprise, is left discreetly obscure.

Shaw's reasons for creating the obscurity are clear, however, and we can appreciate the difficulty he faced. He had to include the words "strangely innocent relations" because that was what he had assured Charlotte his relations with Stella had actually been. He also had to include the words to avoid legal proceedings from Stella, who wrote, as soon as she learned of the scene, "You have no legal right to put me in a play without my knowledge, or permission—damn you!" He had to include them, finally, because he was reluctant to tell an outright lie albeit quite willing to misrepresent in order to enhance his public image and to continue his campaign of revenge. The implication of the scene is that Orinthia is indeed the King's mistress, but the passing words "strangely innocent relations" allow Shaw the security of having it both ways. Nevertheless, with one eye on protecting himself, he is unable to focus on the implausibility of the scene even apart from its inorganic relation to the play as a whole. That implausibility derives more from what he leaves out than what he puts in. He includes part of the skeleton of his relationship with Mrs. Campbell, but he omits its heart. He excludes the overwhelming appeal that she had once had for him, an appeal based not only on her beauty but also on her "manifold nature," as he called it. He excludes her occupation; and, after all, it had been her gifts as a diligent, self-supporting actress which had first captivated him. Orinthia is merely a parasitic and self-indulgent trifler, devoid of Mrs. Campbell's strength of character. By portraying Stella in ways that allowed him to vindicate his hostility and to rationalize once again his past behavior, he ends up with a hollow woman who discredits her royal patron. Shaw thinks he is displaying the King's superiority and creating sympathy for a long-suffering male, but he forces us to conclude that Magnus is a fool to put up with the situation.

This error by the dramatist, as we may recall, corresponds to the one in *Man and Superman,* where the relative implausibility of the romance between Tanner and Ann can be traced to Shaw's need to avenge himself on Charlotte and to deny that he had pursued her. Now once again, in belittling a woman who had disappointed him, he leaves out the feelings that had drawn him to her. In both instances, his attempts to restore his ego lessened his ability to recapture the emotions that preceded the defeat. That here, in contrast to his earlier play, he scarcely disguised the identity of the woman, and in fact quickly made it known, indicates his eagerness to have people believe that the relationship between Magnus and Orinthia duplicated his own with Stella, so that their letters when published would be interpreted in ways favorable to himself; like Magnus, he would appear the victim of a scheming woman whose efforts to break up his marriage he had nobly resisted. And this interpretation is precisely the one that was later to be purveyed by some of Shaw's biographers, such as St. John Ervine.

There were also the more immediate satisfactions of humiliating Stella in person. At the end of March 1929, soon after finishing a draft of the play, Shaw wrote to taunt her with the Orinthia scene. "Perhaps you will never speak to me again when you have read it—or seen it," he said. He excused himself as "too shy" to read the scene to her, but urged her to learn its exact contents from a mutual friend who had recently heard him give a private reading. When that friend reported to Mrs.

Campbell her recollection of the "Interlude" but apparently forgot its ending, Shaw gloatingly informed Stella that the ending was "of the red hot poker order: wildly disgraceful." (The ending of his preceding play, *Saint Joan,* was hotter, with Joan burning at the stake—but now Shaw seems to have switched from the victim's side to the persecutor's.) To make sure that Stella had heard him correctly, he wrote in another letter "that the scene is amusingly scandalous and even disgraceful." The scandal and disgrace, as they both knew, would be entirely hers, and the amusement entirely his. She was distressed by what she termed the "tricks" of her friend. "You are out of tune with friendship and simple courtesy," she told him, and urged him again to let her read the play. For three months he managed to evade her, allowing the work to be premiered intact in Warsaw. Then, when he finally visited and read the scene, it seems to have been only to refine the game he was making her play, for after inserting a few changes, far fewer than she requested, he told her, "I shall now be able to say that you revised it yourself, and dictated some of the best bits." Her continued protests against the "vulgarity and untruthfulness" of the scene had no effect. But perhaps concerned over her threats to charge him with libel, he kept assuring her that "of course the scene isn't true." "There are no personalities in the narrower sense," he held. "Orinthia is not a portrait; she is a study for which you sat as a model in bits only." These reassurances brought no comfort since they were contradicted by an earlier boast: "I have made a superb picture of you, God forgive me! and you must play the game." When he also insisted on his privileges as a writer—"I am an artist and as such unscrupulous when I find my model"—she may have thought that he sounded remarkably like his own Dubedat, the artist as scoundrel. King Magnus had told Orinthia that he sometimes felt the impulse to kick her and that he would even sign her death warrant without turning a hair. But Shaw restrained Magnus's destructive impulses far more than he restrained his own, and despite occasional qualms he allowed the scene to stand without serious change. When the play held its English premiere in Malvern in August, and then began a long subsequent run in London, Stella Campbell had to bear the humiliation as best she could.

Yet although Stella's pleas failed to move Shaw, her final advice to him before the play opened was right in all but one particular: "Tear it up, and re-write it with every scrap of the mischevious vulgarian omitted, and all the suburban backchat against Charlotte and suggested harlotry against me, and the inference of your own superiority wiped out. People will only say that old age and superhuman vanity have robbed you of your commonsense." Stella's mistake was simply that Shaw's common sense had long since deserted him in his attitude toward her. His vindictiveness had first appeared several years earlier when he wrote the postscript to *Pygmalion,* and Eliza's supposed hope of knocking Higgins off his pedestal and forcing him to make love to her was now partially fulfilled in Orinthia's grappling on the floor with a reluctant Magnus. Similarly, Eliza's debasement in the postscript was paralleled by the debasing of Orinthia. "The Interlude" in *The Apple Cart* was thus merely the latest and most direct of Shaw's attacks on Stella, and it was not to be the last! For the final act of Shaw's revenge, at once the strangest and most self-defeating of them all, came when he altered *Pygmalion* itself; and having witnessed the other phases of the campaign we are now ready to view the spectacle of the artist desecrating his own living masterpiece.

VI

The revisions to *Pygmalion* were made during the 1930s, chiefly in 1934 for the following year's German film produced by Eberhard Klagemann, and then again for the 1938 English film produced by Gabriel Pascal. Shaw drew on this material, especially the 1934 additions, when he issued in 1941 a revised text of the play designed to support his changed attitude toward Eliza and Higgins. We will briefly attend to the five added scenes and to some of the small verbal changes. Almost all of this new material expresses the same mood that had incited the attack on Stella as Orinthia. With Eliza Doolittle now once again the substitute target for Stella, as in the postscript, the campaign of revenge reaches its culminating cruelty. Shaw torments Eliza as soon as he can get his hands on her, putting her into three separate torture chambers in the very first three of the added scenes.

In the first of these, at the end of act 1, we follow Eliza's taxi to her lodgings and hear the taximan humiliate her by refusing to accept her money and by laughing at her. She then trudges up the alley to her small room, which is lined with "very old wall paper hanging loose in the damp places." A broken window pane is mended only with paper, an empty birdcage hangs in front of it, and "the rest is the irreducible minimum of poverty's needs: a wretched bed heaped with all sorts of coverings that have any warmth in them, a draped packing case with a basin and jug on it and a little looking glass over it, a chair and table, the refuse of some suburban kitchen." The scene ends as Eliza removes her skirt and shoes and climbs into bed to keep warm. Years earlier Shaw would have presented these details in order to comment on the misery of the poor under capitalism; but now the description is at best neutrally offered and, more likely we may suspect, with some joy in Eliza's predicament.

Our suspicions are confirmed when we see Eliza arrive in the next act at Higgins's house, and the added scene shows Mrs. Pearce preparing the terrified girl for a bath. Eliza protests with tears when she sees the tub, and Mrs. Pearce—no longer protective as in the original version—further humiliates the girl by calling her a "dirty slut" and a "frowsy slut." Commanded to undress, Eliza briefly disappears from view while Mrs. Pearce fills the bath and readies it for "her prisoner"; she lathers from a ball of soap "a formidable looking long handled scrubbing brush," and then:

> *Eliza comes back with nothing on but the bath gown huddled tightly round her, a piteous spectacle of abject terror.*
>
> MRS. PEARCE: Now come along. Take that thing off.
>
> LIZA: Oh I couldnt, Mrs. Pearce: I reely couldnt. I never done such a thing.
>
> MRS. PEARCE: Nonsense. Here: step in and tell me whether its hot enough for you.
>
> LIZA: Ah-oo! Ah-oo! It's too hot.
>
> MRS. PEARCE [*deftly snatching the gown away and throwing Eliza down on her back*]: It wont hurt you. [*She sets to work with the scrubbing brush.*]
>
> *Eliza's screams are heartrending.*

One may wonder if the old playwright's heart was rent at all. Perhaps some other part of his body was in small measure stirred as he vicariously snatched the gown from the nude girl, threw her down on her back, and set to work with that stiff, formidable looking, long handled brush lathered from its ball of soap! (Elsewhere in the play, and unchanged from the original version, reference is made to the bath's "wooden bowl of soap"; Shaw misremembers this as a "ball" while creating a disguised act of rape; and the "long handled" brush may carry an unintended personal conjunction with Higgins's possible onanism.) Yet even if the cleaning up of Eliza's body does not hint at impurities in Shaw's own mind, whatever appeal the scene may have is manifestly sadistic; despite Shaw's announcements of a "heartrending" and "a piteous spectacle," we are not really meant to feel sympathy for Eliza's plight. And curiously, the last spoken line of the scene, assuring Eliza that she won't be hurt, is practically the same as Higgins's first line of the play ("Who's hurting you, you silly girl?"), and we saw earlier that this disclaimer in no way prevents Higgins from tormenting Eliza. The sadism that Shaw had once exposed in Higgins is now practiced by the playwright himself, who shows again as he had in the postscript how much he is embracing Higgins's worst traits. Indeed, one almost fancies that Higgins is now the playwright, and a careless one too, for in Shaw's lust to torture Eliza in the hot bath he forgets that later on in the play, and left intact from the original version, Eliza describes her bath as having been a treat for her, with "soft brushes to scrub yourself," "woolly towels," and soap "smelling like primroses." The inconsistency is not in itself of much importance, but the difference between these two versions of Eliza in the bath—the once pleasant experience turned into the opposite—underscores the change in Shaw's attitude.

The third added scene carries us to yet another torture chamber, the professor's laboratory, as Eliza receives her initial lesson in pronunciation. Shaw again sees to it that she is quickly brought to tears:

> HIGGINS: Now do you think you could possibly say tea? Not ta-yee, mind: if you ever say ba-yee ca-yee da-yee again you shall be dragged round the room three times by the hair of your head. [*Fortissimo*] T, T, T, T.
>
> LIZA [*weeping*]: I cant hear no difference cep that it sounds more genteel-like when you say it.
>
> HIGGINS: Well, if you can hear that difference, what the devil are you crying for? Pickering: give her a chocolate.
>
> PICKERING: No, no. Never mind crying a little, Miss Doolittle: you are doing very well; and the lessons wont hurt. I promise you I wont let him drag you round the room by your hair.
>
> HIGGINS: Be off with you to Mrs. Pearce and tell her about it. Think about it. Try to do it by yourself: and keep your tongue well forward in your mouth instead of trying to roll it up and swallow it. Another lesson at half-past four this afternoon. Away with you.
>
> *Eliza, still sobbing, rushes from the room.*
>
> And that is the sort of ordeal poor Eliza has to go through for months.

Higgins clearly need not drag her by her hair since the playwright secures the same effect on her by the ordeal he has staged, and it is equally clear that her tears differ from the crocodile tears which drip from Shaw's eyes. So intent is he on hurting Eliza that he unwittingly turns Higgins into an inept teacher who depends on Pickering to prevent her from running away. This we may feel cannot be the Henry Higgins who had taught scores of American millionairesses to speak English.

The same regrettable coarsening of Shaw's taste and judgment, if not the same display of sadism, is also evident in the two other added scenes—the Embassy scene at the end of act 3 and Eliza's meeting with Freddy at the end of act 4. Neither need detain us, and Higgins might well have been the playwright here since neither scene rises above a pedestrian level. At the Embassy reception, for example, the professor meets a bewhiskered former pupil and present rival named Nepommuck:

> NEPOMMUCK: I am your pupil: your first pupil, your best and greatest pupil. I am little Nepommuck, the marvellous boy. I have made your name famous throughout Europe. You teach me phonetic. You cannot forget ME.
>
> HIGGINS: Why dont you shave?
>
> NEPOMMUCK: I have not your imposing appearance, your chin, your brow. Nobody notice me when I shave. Now I am famous: they call me Hairy Faced Dick.

And so in the same vein. When Shaw has to bid for a laugh with a "Hairy Faced Dick" we feel a strain which distresses all the more for the contrasting ease of the humor in the original version. Feeble in itself, the scene also damages the great midnight encounter between Eliza and Higgins in act 4, robbing it of its suspense.

Also damaging is the revision of the end of that act, which had once concluded with a superb bit of pantomime showing the complexity of Eliza's feelings after she had infuriated Higgins and driven him from the room:

> *Eliza smiles for the first time; expresses her feelings by a wild pantomime in which an imitation of Higgins's exit is confused with her own triumph; and finally goes down on her knees on the hearthrug to look for the ring.*

And then we later learn that she spends most of the night wandering the streets of London alone, depressed to the verge of suicide. In the new version Eliza is not allowed to enjoy her moment of triumph:

> *Eliza goes down on her knees on the hearthrug to look for the ring.*

> *When she finds it she considers for a moment what to do with it. Finally she flings it down on the dessert stand and goes upstairs in a tearing rage.*

At this point Shaw adds a two-part scene as Eliza goes to her room, changes her clothes (with Shaw arranging for the third time in the new scenes to disrobe her), sticks out her tongue at herself in a mirror, and then leaves the house. Outside she runs into the lovelorn Freddy Hill who had been standing vigil beneath her window. They chat briefly, embrace and kiss, are interrupted by a police constable, flee to Cavendish Square, embrace and kiss, are interrupted by another constable, flee to Hanover Square, embrace and kiss, are interrupted by a passing taximan, and then ride off to spend the rest of the night apparently in the cab. The effect of this facetious scene, replete with improbabilities, is to lessen Eliza's dignity and to make Freddy a fool. In turning Eliza's once desperate flight from Higgins into farce, Shaw exposes how completely he has withdrawn from her the sympathy of the original version and has substituted the hostility of the postscript. Scenes free of such hostility might have been added to the play, but the ones we are given are not merely inferior in quality but upset the fine balance of the entirety. It attests to the strength of the play that it still can bear the weight of these gross additions.

Shaw also tinkers with the play in smaller ways, guided by the determination to embarrass Eliza, to rehabilitate Higgins, and to make the work conform to the changed perspectives of the postscript. Higgins now condemns Eliza's future husband Freddy as a fool not even good enough to get a job as an errand boy—exactly the same term as was first used in the postscript. The end of Eliza's line, "I'll marry Freddy, I will, as soon as he's able to support me," is changed to "as soon as I'm able to support him." New words of abuse are heaped upon Eliza as she is called a "squashed cabbage leaf" and an "incarnate insult to the English language." Contrastingly, Shaw now deletes Higgins's boast that he writes poetry "on Miltonic lines" and also deletes Higgins's words that "we are all dependent on one another, every soul of us on earth," while leaving intact his claim that he could "do without anybody." These niggling alterations—and there are others—are merely symptomatic of the change in Shaw's outlook and damage the play far less than the added scenes. But Shaw's final bit of tinkering, at the very end of the work, does create a significant shift in the audience's response. We recall that in the original ending Eliza bids farewell to her professor and tells him that she will not see him again; but when his mother offers to shop for the tie and gloves he had just ordered Eliza to buy for him, he confidently tells her not to bother:

> HIGGINS [*sunnily*]: Oh, dont bother. She'll buy em all right enough. Goodbye.
> *They kiss, Mrs. Higgins runs out. Higgins, left alone, rattles his cash in his pocket, chuckles; and disports himself in a highly self-satisfied manner.*

This ending leaves open the possibility of Eliza's return. But if she does not return then the joke would be on the smug Higgins. In the new ending, however, Shaw tries to turn the joke against Eliza, who is now to be burdened with the incompetent Freddy Hill:

> LIZA: What you are to do without me I cannot imagine. [*She sweeps out.*]
> MRS. HIGGINS: I'm afraid youve spoilt that girl, Henry. I should be uneasy about you and her if she were less fond of Colonel Pickering.
> HIGGINS: Pickering! Nonsense: she's going to marry Freddy. Ha ha! Freddy! Freddy!! ha ha ha ha ha!!!!! [*He roars with laughter as the play ends.*]

The contemptuous laughter, hard and dead, is Shaw's very own. And with this change in the ending, similar in mood to all of the other revisions, the playwright completed his work of superimposing on the play an entirely different attitude toward his leading characters. Not a single one of the changes had improved the script in the slightest; all had damaged it in greater or lesser measure; and actors today who perform the play might be well advised to stay with the marvelous original version rather than to follow the angry old dramatist in profaning it. A work of art written in love cannot be successfully revised in hate, and Shaw's latter-day hostility to the play shows through in every touch he added. It had become an accusing mirror reflecting his past self, and to meet his current personal needs he splattered the mirror with ink. He may have sensed that he was abusing the play but he did not care. What he might have cared about, had he been able to recognize it, was the degree to which his own sensitivity to language had hardened; for if one compares any of the new dialogue to that of the original, the discordance between the two—the vulgarization of the rhythms and the diction—is immediately apparent. Thus the most damning price Shaw paid for his changed attitude toward Eliza was his inability to hear the sound of her voice, and it is ironic indeed to find the man who in later life was so concerned with phonetics becoming almost stone-deaf himself to the music of language.

Chronology

1856	Born on July 26, in Dublin, Ireland.
1876	Moves to London in the hopes of professional advancement and becomes a small-time journalist.
1879	Hired by the Edison Telephone Company and completes his first novel, *Immaturity.*
1880	Writes a second novel, *The Irrational Knot.* Joins the Dialectical Society.
1881	Becomes a vegetarian in an attempt to cure migraine headaches and takes lessons in boxing. Writes *Love among the Artists.*
1882	Converts to socialism and completes his best novel, *Cashel Byron's Profession.*
1884	Falls among the Fabians. *An Unsocial Socialist* is serialized.
1885	Father dies.
1886–88	Works as an art critic and music critic for various journals.
1889	Publishes *Fabian Essays.*
1890	Begins work as a music critic for *The World.* Lectures to the Fabian Society on Ibsen.
1891	Publishes *The Quintessence of Ibsenism.*
1892–93	*Widowers' Houses, The Philanderer, Mrs Warren's Profession.*
1894	*Arms and the Man, Candida.*
1895	Starts as drama critic for the *Saturday Review. The Man of Destiny, You Never Can Tell.*
1896	*The Devil's Disciple.*
1898	Marries Charlotte Payne-Townshend. *Caesar and Cleopatra, The Perfect Wagnerite.*
1899	*Captain Brassbound's Conversion.*
1903	*Man and Superman.*
1904	*John Bull's Other Island.*

1905	Visits Ireland. *Major Barbara.*
1906	Meets Ellen Terry. *The Doctor's Dilemma, Our Theatre in the Nineties.*
1908	*Getting Married.*
1909	*Misalliance, The Shewing-up of Blanco Posnet.*
1911	*Fanny's First Play.*
1912	*Androcles and the Lion, Pygmalion.* Friendship with Mrs. Patrick Campbell.
1914	*Common Sense About the War.*
1916–19	*Heartbreak House.*
1920	*Back to Methuselah.*
1923	*Saint Joan.*
1926	Receives the Nobel Prize for literature—uses the prize money to support the publication of translations from Swedish literature.
1928	*The Intelligent Woman's Guide to Socialism, Capitalism, Sovietism, and Fascism.*
1929	*The Apple Cart.*
1931	*Ellen Terry and Bernard Shaw: A Correspondence.* Travels to U.S.S.R.
1932	*The Adventures of the Black Girl in Her Search for God.*
1933	Goes to America.
1934	*Collected Prefaces.*
1939	*In Good King Charles's Golden Days.*
1943	Wife dies.
1944	*Everybody's Political What's What.*
1950	Dies on November 13.

Contributors

HAROLD BLOOM, Sterling Professor of the Humanities at Yale University, is the author of *The Anxiety of Influence, Poetry and Repression,* and many other volumes of literary criticism. His forthcoming study, *Freud: Transference and Authority,* attempts a full-scale reading of all of Freud's major writings. A MacArthur Prize Fellow, he is general editor of five series of literary criticism published by Chelsea House. During 1987–88, he served as the Charles Eliot Norton Professor of Poetry at Harvard University.

ERIC BENTLEY is widely regarded as one of the foremost literary critics of modern drama. His books include *The Playwright as Thinker* and *Bernard Shaw 1856–1950.* He is currently Professor of Comparative Literature at the University of Maryland.

NIGEL ALEXANDER is the author of *A Critical Commentary on* Arms and the Man *and* Pygmalion.

LOUIS CROMPTON is Professor of English at the University of Nebraska. He is the author of *Shaw the Dramatist* and writes extensively on homosexual literature and history. His most recent book is *Byron and Greek Love: Homophobia in 19th Century England.*

CHARLES A. BERST is Professor of English at the University of California at Los Angeles. He is the author of *Bernard Shaw and the Art of Drama* and the editor of *Shaw and Religion.*

LISË PEDERSEN is Associate Professor of English at Tennessee State University.

ERROL DURBACH is Professor of English at the University of British Columbia and the author of *Ibsen the Romantic: Analogues of Paradise in the Later Plays.*

ARTHUR GANZ is Professor of English at the City College of New York and the author of *George Bernard Shaw* and *Realms of the Self: Variations on a Theme in Modern Drama*.

ARNOLD SILVER is Professor of English at the University of Massachusetts and the author of *Shaw: The Darker Side*.

Bibliography

Adams, Elsie B. *Bernard Shaw and the Aesthetes*. Columbus: Ohio State University Press, 1971.

Beardsmore, Hugo Baetens. "A Sociolinguistic Interpretation of *Pygmalion*." *English Studies* 60 (1979): 712–19.

Bentley, Eric. *The Playwright as Thinker.* New York: Reynal & Hitchcock, 1946.

Briden, E. F. "James's Miss Churm: Another of Eliza's Prototypes?" *Shaw Review* 19 (1976): 17–21.

Chesterton, G. K. *George Bernard Shaw.* Hill & Wang, 1956.

Costello, Donald P. *The Serpent's Eye: Shaw and the Cinema*. Notre Dame, Ind.: University of Notre Dame Press, 1965.

Crane, Milton. "*Pygmalion:* Bernard Shaw's Dramatic Theory and Practice." *PMLA* 66 (1951): 879–85.

Dent, Alan, ed. *Bernard Shaw and Mrs Patrick Campbell: Their Correspondence*. New York: AMS Press, 1952.

Dukore, Bernard F. *Bernard Shaw, Director.* Seattle: University of Washington Press, 1971.

———. *Bernard Shaw, Playwright: Aspects of Shavian Drama*. Columbia: University of Missouri Press, 1973.

Ervine, St. John. *Shaw: His Life, Work, and Friends*. New York: Morrow, 1972.

Evans, T. F., ed. *Shaw: The Critical Heritage*. London: Routledge & Kegan Paul, 1976.

Gibbs, A. M. *The Art and Mind of Shaw.* London: Macmillan, 1983.

Goldberg, Michael. "Shaw's *Pygmalion:* The Reworking of *Great Expectations*." *Shaw Review* 22 (1979): 114–22.

Harris, Edward P. "The Liberation of Flesh from Stone: *Pygmalion* in Frank Wedekind's *Erdgeist*." *The Germanic Review* 52 (1977): 44–56.

Harris, Frank. *Bernard Shaw.* Garden City, N.Y.: Garden City Publishing, 1931.

Holroyd, Michael, ed. *The Genius of Shaw: A Symposium*. New York: Holt, Rinehart & Winston, 1979.

Huggett, Richard. *The Truth about* Pygmalion. London: Heinemann, 1969.

Irvine, William. *The Universe of G. B. S.* New York: Whittlesey House, 1949.

Laurence, Dan H., ed. *Letters of George Bernard Shaw.* 3 vols. New York: Viking, 1985.

Lauter, Paul. "*Candida* and *Pygmalion:* Shaw's Subversion of Stereotypes." *Shaw Review* 3 (1960): 14–19.

Lorichs, Sonja. *The Unwomanly Woman in Bernard Shaw's Drama and Her Social and Political Background.* University of Uppsala Studies in English, no. 15. Uppsala, Sweden: Almqvist & Wiksell, 1973.

MacCarthy, Desmond. *Shaw: The Plays.* London: MacGibbon & Kee, 1951.

Matlaw, Myron. "Will Higgins Marry Eliza?" *Shavian* 1, no. 12 (1958): 14–19.

Meisel, Martin. *Shaw and the Nineteenth-Century Theater.* Princeton, N.J.: Princeton University Press, 1963.

Mills, John A. *Language and Laughter: Comic Diction in the Plays of Bernard Shaw.* Tucson: University of Arizona Press, 1969.

Morgan, Margery M. "Edwardian Feminism and the Drama: Shaw and Granville Barker." *Cahiers Victoriens & Edouardiens* 9/10 (1979): 63–85.

Nethercot, Arthur H. *Men and Supermen: The Shavian Portrait Gallery.* New York: Blom, 1966.

O'Donnell, Norbert F. "On the 'Unpleasantness' of *Pygmalion.*" *Shaw Bulletin* 1, no. 2 (1955): 7–10.

O'Donovan, John. *G. B. Shaw.* Dublin: Gill & Macmillan, 1983.

Ohmann, Richard M. *Shaw: The Style and the Man.* Middletown, Conn.: Wesleyan University Press, 1962.

Quinn, Martin. "The Informing Presence of Charles Dickens in Bernard Shaw's *Pygmalion.*" *Dickensian* 80 (1984): 144–50.

Rattray, R. F. "The Subconscious and Shaw." *Quarterly Review* 291 (1953): 210–22.

Schotter, Richard D. "Shaw's Stagecraft: A Theatrical Study of *Pygmalion.*" Ph.D. diss., Columbia University, 1974.

Silver, Arnold. *Bernard Shaw: The Darker Side.* Stanford: Stanford University Press, 1982.

Smith, Percy J. *The Unrepentant Pilgrim.* Boston: Houghton Mifflin, 1965.

Solomon, Stanley J. "The Ending of *Pygmalion:* A Structural View." *Educational Theatre Journal* 16 (1964): 59–63.

Strauss, Emil. *Bernard Shaw: Art and Socialism.* Darby, Pa.: Folcroft Library Editions, 1942.

Turco, Alfred, Jr. *Shaw's Moral Vision: The Self and Salvation.* Ithaca, N.Y.: Cornell University Press, 1976.

Valency, Maurice. *The Cart and the Trumpet: The Plays of George Bernard Shaw.* New York: Oxford University Press, 1973.

Weintraub, Rodelle. *Fabian Feminist: Bernard Shaw and Woman.* University Park: Pennsylvania State University Press, 1977.

West, Alick. *George Bernard Shaw: "A Good Man Fallen Among Fabians."* New York: International Publishers, 1950.

Wilson, Colin. *Bernard Shaw: A Reassessment.* London: Hutchinson, 1969.

Wisenthal, J. L. *The Marriage of Contraries: Bernard Shaw's Middle Plays.* Cambridge: Harvard University Press, 1974.

Woodbridge, Homer E. *George Bernard Shaw: Creative Artist.* Carbondale: Southern Illinois University Press, 1963.

Acknowledgments

"A Personal Play" (originally entitled "*Pygmalion*") by Eric Bentley from *Bernard Shaw 1856–1950* by Eric Bentley, © 1947, 1957 by New Directions Publishing Co., © renewed 1975 by Eric Bentley. Reprinted by permission of Proscenium Publishers, Inc.

"The Play of Ideas" (originally entitled "*Pygmalion*") by Nigel Alexander from *A Critical Commentary on Bernard Shaw's* Arms and the Man *and* Pygmalion by Nigel Alexander, © 1968 by Nigel Alexander. Reprinted by permission of Macmillan & Co. Ltd.

"Improving *Pygmalion*" (originally entitled "*Pygmalion*") by Louis Crompton from *Shaw the Dramatist* by Louis Crompton, © 1969 by the University of Nebraska Press. Reprinted by permission of the University of Nebraska Press.

"*Pygmalion:* A Potboiler as Art" by Charles A. Berst from *Bernard Shaw and the Art of Drama* by Charles A. Berst, © 1973 by the Board of Trustees of the University of Illinois. Reprinted by permission of the University of Illinois Press.

"Shakespeare's *The Taming of the Shrew* vs. Shaw's *Pygmalion:* Male Chauvinism vs. Women's Lib?" by Lisë Pedersen from *Fabian Feminist: Bernard Shaw and Woman,* edited by Rodelle Weintraub, © 1977 by Pennsylvania State University. Reprinted by permission of Pennsylvania State University Press, University Park, Pennsylvania.

"Pygmalion: Myth and Anti-Myth in the Plays of Ibsen and Shaw" by Errol Durbach from *English Studies in Africa* 21, no. 1 (March 1978), © 1978 by Witwatersrand University Press. Reprinted by permission.

"The Problematic Ending of *Pygmalion*" (originally entitled "Plays of Maturity") by Arthur Ganz from *George Bernard Shaw* by Arthur Ganz, © 1983 by Arthur Ganz. Reprinted by permission of Macmillan & Co. Ltd.

"The Playwright's Revenge" by Arnold Silver from *Bernard Shaw—The Darker Side* by Arnold Silver, © 1982 by the Board of Trustees of the Leland Stanford Junior University. Reprinted by permission of the publishers, Stanford University Press.

Index